REVIE

M000010357

"Happiness is one of the most powerful advantages in a student's life, yet it is often overlooked or feels too ambitious in the midst of challenge. In STRIVE, Robert Dunlop makes a clear case for why happiness is a crucial component of achieving our potential and provides practical ways to use happiness to help schools flourish--not just for a few lucky teachers and students, but for the rest of us as well."

— SHAWN ACHOR
NY Times bestselling author
Happiness Advantage, Before Happiness & *Big Potential*

"This book is a gem for teachers looking to be professionally engaged and personally rejuvenated! The STRIVE acronym provides a useful framework to build the wellbeing of teachers and students. The book encourages self reflection and offers concrete exercises that will impact your daily life at school."

— LEA WATERS (PHD)
author of *The Strength Switch*
President of the International Positive Psychology Association

"I thoroughly enjoyed reading Strive for Happiness in Education by Robert Dunlop. As a former educator and now a positive psychology practitioner, I feel that this book is well-researched but more importantly, simplifies the science of human flourishing in a way that can easily be applied to the lives of busy teachers."

— PATRICE PALMER
author of *The Teacher Self-Care Manual*

"Strive is packed with practical, insightful, and engaging strategies that you can start using in your classroom today, tomorrow, and for years to come. Strive will leave you smiling and empowered to find new pathways to happiness in your work."

— MICHAEL SNOW
Educator, Grade 5

"This is a must read for any educator at any stage of their career. We cannot be at our best as teachers without feeling vital, purposeful, fulfilled and happy. This book teaches us that we are responsible for our own efficacy and teaches us how to positively impact our efficacy - for the betterment of our students' lives and our own."

- KIM DESING-MCCARDLE
Literacy Consultant, Grade 9-12

"STRIVE goes beyond traditional teaching handbooks to help educators understand how to make meaning from relationships within the profession, and the profession itself, in order to achieve greater personal happiness throughout a career. It is a powerful read for both new and experienced teachers providing useful resources and practical self analysis tools!

Rob's warmth and candor will keep readers engaged in this reflective and timely resource that provides numerous opportunities for both personal and staff professional development."

- MELISSA MCKINNEY-LEPP
Educator, STEAM

Susan.

STRIVE

for happiness in education.

You deserve it!

Rob Dunlop

Published by EduMatch®
PO Box 150324, Alexandria, VA 22315
www.edumatchpublishing.com

These books are available at special discounts when purchased in quantities of 10 or more for use as premiums, promotions fundraising, and educational use.

For inquiries and details, contact the publisher:
sarah@edumatch.org.

ISBN: 978-1-970133-57-8

educational matchmaker

To all educators, who work endlessly
to support and love students.

CONTENT

Preface   11

PART ONE: HAPPINESS

The Power of Happiness.............................   19
Preparing for Happiness............................   25
Working Towards Happiness.......................   33

PART TWO: STRIVE

S STUDENTS
Deep Connections   43
Those Who Need Us the Most.............   57

T TEAM
Teach Friends Forever.......................   71
Positive Personal Learning Networks   85

R ROUTINES
Nudges, Triggers and Cues   99
Teacher Happiness Routines   109

I INNOVATE
Where, Who, What and When   181
How We Teach.................................   193

V VIABILITY
Peaks and Valleys.............................   205
Navigating Through Stress................   217

E EXTRAORDINARY
Be the One......................................   229

STRIVE

(def.) to make great efforts to achieve or obtain something.

PREFACE

"Maybe you are searching among the branches, for what only appears in the roots."
— *Rumi*

A retired school teacher planted a tree in her backyard that did not thrive. As she was bringing it to the curb, the children who lived next door approached her and asked, "What happened to the tree?"

Always looking for a teachable moment, she turned the question back to them. Immediately, the children noticed the leaves. They were dry, brown, and becoming brittle. Within minutes, they came to the conclusion that the reason the tree did not survive was because the leaves were not healthy.

She applauded their initial observations and explained to them that the leaves are very important for the tree to stay healthy, however, it was not the reason this tree was unable to survive. She challenged them to think of other issues that could have impacted this tree.

They thought about it, and then the young girl asked where the tree was planted. This led them to the hole in the backyard where the tree had been. Their focus shifted to the environment that surrounded the tree. At first, they discussed the amount of sun and shade that the tree was exposed to and how this would affect its growth. She told them that they were getting close and encouraged them to keep thinking.

It did not take long for the young boy to start playing in the dirt that surrounded the tree. He noticed that this dirt was a lot different from the soil in the gardens at his house. It was much harder and claylike. The neighbor educated them on the different types of soil and explained to them that the soil is where trees and plants get the essential nutrients they need.

Both children soon became fixated on how the roots of the tree would be able to spread through this hard soil. They formulated another hypothesis explaining that the soil in which the tree was planted had the greatest impact on this tree's ability to thrive. The neighbor applauded and confirmed their discovery.

By digging deeper, they were able to get to the root of the issue. The children were excited by this new knowledge and wondered what changes would be necessary for a new tree to grow healthy and strong in this backyard.

There are significant parallels between this tree inquiry and education. As a system, we tend to be very leaf focused. We are drawn to data, just like these children were drawn to the leaves. This is our indicator of how our students are achieving. It is a very important aspect of education; however, it does not always lead us to what our students need most to grow.

Trying to fix one leaf at a time will never yield us the result that we are looking for. It might give us temporary gains in very specific areas; however, it will not lead to sustainable growth. We need to dig deeper and invest more in determining the underlying reasons that students are struggling. The greater our ability to understand our students' emotional needs, the better chance we have to help them learn.

For instance, social-emotional learning (SEL) is the process of helping students understand and manage their emotions. It also focuses on setting goals, showing empathy, culturing relationships and making responsible decisions.[1] Many schools around the world are implementing SEL programs, and the research supports their effectiveness. A meta-analysis of over 270,000 students showed an 11% increase on achievement tests when social-emotional learning was embedded in their education.[2]

By looking beyond the leaves and getting to the root of the issues, we are providing students with the education and support they need to be successful beyond just academics. This will better prepare them for the future and help them in all aspects of their lives.

As a system, we often take a leaf-focused approach to supporting educators. We believe that to improve the quality of teachers, we need to focus on teaching strategies. I acknowledge that these strategies are very vital to the success of the system; however, we need to ask ourselves, "What has the greatest impact on teacher performance?"

If you are willing to dig deeper, you will discover that it is teacher happiness. There is nothing more important than creating a culture in education in which teachers love being teachers. We need to work together to create a profession that is awesome to be a part of. One that people enter inspired and leave inspired. One that can be felt when we walk into the building. One that lets students see what achieving joy through work looks like each day. To do this, we must look beyond the leaves to discover — or rediscover — where true happiness lies in education.

My Why Behind This Book

I set out on a journey to write this book because, at times in my career, I have struggled to maintain my passion and love of teaching. I vividly recall sitting alone in the principal's office, preparing to shut down completely and ready to be that teacher who dreams of nothing more than retirement. This is something that I am not proud of, but something I feel is too common in education.

Thankfully, I met a teacher named Wendy Bilinski, who showed me that it is possible to stay happy and motivated throughout an entire career. Prior to meeting Wendy, we exchanged several emails to set up a time to work together. I mistook her energy and excitement in those emails for that of a young 'go getter' looking to make a name for herself in our district. Expecting a new teacher, I was shocked the first time we met. Wendy had been teaching for 28 years at that point, and her love of education was very clear.

With her red hair and spunky personality, she enthusiastically welcomed me into her class. Her thirst for new learning was evident by her rush to get started. She loved to find new ways to engage her students and deliver learning to them in ways that were meaningful and effective. Wendy's energy was so infectious that I remember driving out of the parking lot saying to myself, "That is what I want to be like that many years into teaching!"

After that day, I could not get Wendy's level of motivation out of my mind. Being in a central role at the time and working with hundreds of teachers every month, I began to become more aware of others in the profession who were able to maintain this level of commitment in teaching.

The decision to write a book occurred after a presentation I was giving to future educators at a local university on "Engaging Students in Learning." It dawned on me mid-presentation that it would be more valuable to help these students learn how to maintain their own level of engagement in education, just as Wendy had. If they could accomplish this, then all other aspects of great teaching would develop naturally and fall into place.

Initially, I set out to write a book on teacher motivation. I began to interview teachers and read as much as possible on this subject. However, just like the tree inquiry presented above, I realized that I needed to dig deeper. I discovered that their motivation stemmed from the fact they were happy and loved coming to work every day.

Since that realization, I have immersed myself fully in reading and learning about happiness and positive psychology. I engage in as many conversations as possible with educators who love their jobs, looking for valuable insight into what they do that allows them to stay positive and happy. This book passes on this learning to you, the reader, in hopes that it will help you maintain your love of teaching throughout your entire career.

STRIVE FOR 40

Education presents the opportunity to be the most satisfying career imaginable. With each day, not unlike the one before it, you have what seems to be unlimited chances to change the world one mind at a time. You can create a world inside four walls that you would have loved to experience when you were a student. Most importantly, you will meet the most amazing young people who will change you, care about you, inspire you, and never forget you as long as they live. However, this is just an opportunity, something that not all teachers will experience.

The teachers who leave the profession truly satisfied are the ones who were able to maintain their love and passion regardless of the situations they encounter. They adapt, reinvent, and invest fully into areas of education that bring them true enjoyment. They take control over their own happiness and fulfillment and seize the many great opportunities they are presented with daily.

In *The How of Happiness*, Sonja Lyubomenski reveals one of the most powerful findings in the field of positive psychology. Her research shows that we have control over approximately 40% of our own happiness. Only 10% of our life satisfaction is based on the circumstances we are faced with.[3] This tells us that our happiness is largely in our control in both life and education.

It is essential to note that happiness is not something that you find or achieve, it is something that you constantly strive for. There is always going to be ups and downs. You will face challenges, and you will find success. You will have good days and bad. You will have great classes and ones that take you to your tipping point. The key is to make happiness a priority in education. This is the root of a healthy, fulfilling, and truly impactful career.

PART ONE: HAPPINESS

The Power of Happiness

*"The only way to do great work is
to love the work you do."*
— Steve Jobs

Happiness is now a top priority in many of the biggest corporations in the world. Companies such as Google, Facebook, Proctor and Gamble, and American Express are investing a lot of energy and resources to ensure that their employees enjoy coming to work each day. [4] Whether they are creating inspiring work environments or opportunities for more social interactions and fun, their goal is simple; increase overall contentment amongst their employees.

Some of these companies have even gone as far as hiring Chief Happiness Officers (CHOs) to ensure employee happiness and well-being. This idea was popularized when Google placed Chad-Meng Tan in charge of happiness in one of the most successful companies in the world. [5]

Since then, other companies have followed suit. For instance, CEO of Zappos, Tony Hsieh, wrote a New York Times best seller called Delivering Happiness aimed at increasing morale in the corporate culture. This endeavor was so successful that they now own a consulting firm whose sole focus is to help companies around the world 'deliver happiness' to their employees. Tony stresses to other companies that, "you can't deliver good service from unhappy employees." [6]

Why the shift of corporate leadership and focus? Is this an act of altruism? Do companies just want people to be happy? Definitely not. This is a business decision based primarily on their bottom line. But how does happiness correlate into dollar signs? Productivity!

The Bottom Line

As research emerges in the field of positive psychology, companies are starting to shift their focus in hopes that an improved work culture can result in increased productivity and innovation. They are essentially tapping into the benefits of happiness to give them a corporate edge. Statistics, like the ones below from the Harvard Business Review, are getting the attention of CEOs around the world.[7]

Considering these statistics, it makes sense why companies now have nap pods, hire Chief Happiness Officers, and have begun to make employee happiness a priority. Although these statistics are based on the corporate world, they have remarkable parallels to education.

The People Business

As educators, our business is developing people. Our success lies in our ability to culture relationships, inspire learning, ignite passions, and to build self-efficacy and esteem through our daily interactions with our students. Our success does not result in corner offices, promotions, and raises; it results in changing lives one person at a time.

With this much at stake in education, we must work towards being as productive and effective as possible. And to do that, we need to find and maintain our enjoyment as teachers.

Let's assume that those statistics presented by Harvard would have a similar effect in education. These statistics are focused on human emotion, not the environment that the changes occur in. Their results will be transferable to many facets of life.

31% More Productive

Have you ever met a teacher and thought to yourself, "How do they do it all?" In the classroom, they are constantly trying new things and pushing themselves to be continually better. Then outside the classroom, they are fully immersed in extracurriculars and school initiatives. When you meet them, take time to ask yourself this question, "Are they happy?"

You will find that they are extremely happy. They love what they do, and that is why they do so much. They are driven by passion and a desire to make school an incredible experience for their students. But there still lingers the question, "Where do they get the time?"

Perhaps they are 31% more productive. Think of how much more time we would have each day if we were this productive. Time that could be invested in designing awesome lessons, getting to know students, setting up our classroom, communicating with parents, running extracurriculars, and learning more about our craft as an educator.

With more productivity comes less guilt. Often when we are not productive, we constantly have a laundry list of things we know we need to do, but just can't seem to get to. This tends to wear us down even more, making us feel sluggish and unmotivated. It is like a dark cloud looming over us, making it difficult to enjoy all of the great aspects of teaching and life.

Increasing production is also a great way to help achieve a better work/life balance. Getting what we need done more efficiently will allow us more time to relax and explore our passions and interests outside of work.

23% More Energy

We all know how stress can zap our energy levels and deplete us very quickly. There is no shortage of stress in education, so it is important that we learn to manage this stress if we want to enjoy coming to school each day.

Research shows that having a positive mindset results in 23% greater energy levels in the midst of stress. In addition, stress-related symptoms such as backaches and headaches are also reduced.[8]

The greater our ability to tap into the benefits of being happier, the better we will feel and the more energy we will have to support our students, and do our jobs at a high level.

Three Times More Creative

Done right, there is a lot of creativity that goes into teaching. What great educators do is an art- constantly creating new ways to teach, to adapt, to motivate, to empower, to assess, and to make learning relevant to their students.

Could you imagine if you were three times more creative? What would your lessons look like? How much more fun would you have planning and delivering those lessons? How many more students would look forward to their time with you?

Creativity is needed to help keep the passion alive. Those teachers who are able to maintain their love of teaching are experts at continually changing up how they approach each year. It takes a lot of creativity to find new ways to engage both students and yourself.

37% Higher Sales

Don't get too excited, this part is not going to discuss how you can increase your number of scholastic book orders or sell the most chocolate bars as a class during this year's school fundraiser. Let's focus on what we are selling every day to students that can change their lives.

If we looked at sales in education as student buy-in, could you imagine a 37% increase? What if they bought more into developing a stronger thirst for knowledge, becoming lifelong learners, and developing into the leaders that they have the potential to be? How would that change your classroom? How would that make your interactions with students more fulfilling? How much would that affect your job satisfaction?

When I transfer higher sales into education, I see higher student engagement. Think of those teachers that somehow get students to buy into what they are teaching year after year. Despite the students that enter their room, they seem to have a way of getting most of them to listen and learn from them.

These teachers are successful at getting students to buy-in because they have tapped into the benefits of being happy. They use the 37% increase in productivity, 23% more energy, and triple the amount of creativity to help them become very impactful and inspiring educators.

A Common Misconception

Many of us were raised to believe that the road to happiness starts with hard work. If we put in the time and energy, then eventually success will come. That part I believe is true. It is the next part that is questionable. Once we achieve success, we will then find happiness. Seems logical, but it is a misconception.

In the book The Happiness Advantage, Shawn Achor presents a very strong case that success does not lead to happiness. Living and teaching on the Harvard campus afforded him the luxury of living amongst the most successful academics in America. However, despite their success, many were unhappy.[9]

In 2004, a Harvard Crimson poll found that up to 80% of their students struggled through depression at least once during the school year.[10] In 2006, Harvard offered a course called Positive Psychology (basically happiness), which attracted 1400 students. The school was hoping for 100. This massive interest reinforced that despite their success, students were still in search of happiness.[11]

Even outside the walls of Harvard, we can see countless examples in our everyday lives of people who have worked their way up the ladder, but are none the happier. The Happiness Advantage, as Shawn Achor puts it, presents the idea that we must start with happiness as our goal. This happiness will motivate us to do great work that will eventually lead to our success.

Unacceptable Statistics for Education

In 2013, Gallup surveyed 142 countries on the State of the Global Workplace and found some very unsettling statistics. The poll results showed that only 13% of employees were engaged at work, while 63% reported that they lacked motivation and were less likely to invest extra effort. The remaining 24% indicated that they were unhappy, unproductive and liable to spread negativity to coworkers.[12]

Those are not acceptable statistics for education. Students deserve and need much more. We, as teachers, deserve and need much more. The good news is that happiness is right there waiting for us if we want it.

HAPPINESS H☺MEW☺RK DATE:

1. On the graph provided, draw a line measuring your level of happiness throughout your career. Don't overthink it. Just start on the Y-Axis with how you remember coming into the profession and extend the line higher and lower as you go through each year.

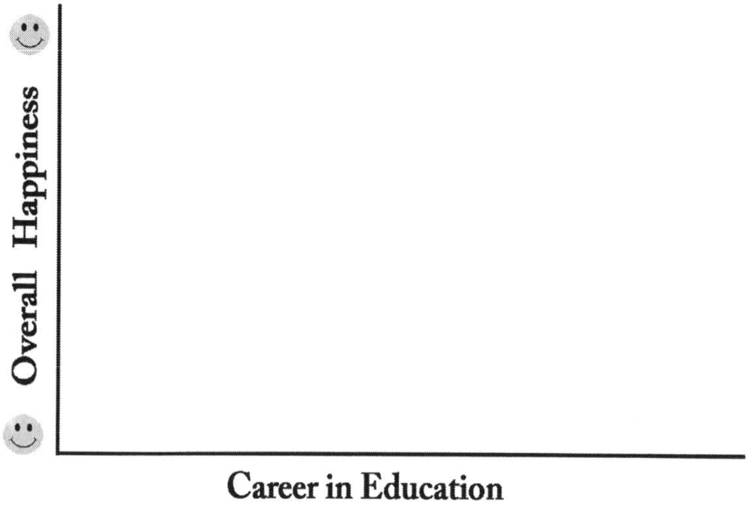
Overall Happiness
Career in Education

2. Circle the happiest years of your career. Reflect on what made these amongst the best for you.

3. Circle the years you struggled the most to be happy. Reflect on what made these years tough to be happy.

4. Are there any trends in which happiness is slowly increasing or decreasing? Why do you feel that these trends occurred?

5. If you are new to teaching, draw a graph anticipating where the peaks and valleys might occur. Reflect on what changes could be made to ensure the valleys are short and meaningful.

Preparing For Happiness

"First, think. Second, believe. Third, dream.
And finally, dare."
— Walt Disney

The first chapter of this book focused on getting you to think about the impact that happiness has on education. But as Walt Disney suggests in the quote above, thinking is just the first step. We need to move beyond thinking to the belief that it is possible for all educators. From there, we can dream about becoming that educator we set out to be and dare to change the world one student at a time.

Let's start by reflecting on your current situation as an educator. Read the following belief statements below and deem if you think they are true or false.

- I believe that all students can learn.
- I believe that I have the ability to positively impact every student's life that I teach.
- I believe that I can be a leader in my school and/or district.
- I believe that change in education starts with me.
- I believe that I can be happy throughout my entire career as a teacher.
- I believe that teaching is the best job for me.

If you were to bring these questions to your next staff meeting, do you think your colleagues would answer these questions the same way? Probably not. Our beliefs are developed through our experiences and our perception of the situations that we experience.

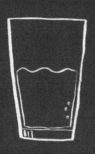

YOUR PERCEPTIONS CREATE YOUR REALITY

CHANGE YOUR PERCEPTIONS TO CHANGE YOUR REALITY

Note the word perception. It is not necessarily the situation that we are in, but it is how we perceive this situation. It is this reality that we create for ourselves that will influence our beliefs.

Same Road, Different Journey

Two teachers are hired at the same time into the same district. They teach a very similar demographic of students and endure the same changes with regard to the expectations and pressures of the system. Both are given similar opportunities to grow as teachers and leaders. Their lives outside are similar in that they both have families, and neither has faced significant tragedy.

Will they both share the same love for teaching at the end of their careers? Will they experience the same highs and lows? Will they share the same struggles and find joy in the same successes? Will their learning lead them down the same path? Probably not.

Every teacher's experience in education is entirely unique. It is a journey based on the daily choices they make, which are governed by their perceptions and beliefs. It is quite possible to have one of these teachers completely fulfilled at the end of their career, while the other is cynical. Yet, both traveled down very similar roads.

Positive Reality

Our brains are inundated with over 11 million bits of information per second. However, the brain is only able to process approximately 50 bits/second.[13] Therefore, it must decide what to let in and what to ignore. The result of this process becomes your reality.

If we are focused primarily on the negative constraints around us, then it will be difficult to have a positive outlook. However, if we are able to focus on the positive opportunities that present themselves, then finding more joy becomes much more attainable.

In Shawn Achor's follow up book, *Before Happiness*, he emphasizes that the best way to change your reality is to realize that there are multiple realities to choose from.[14]

For instance, it is a week before school, and you receive your class list. As you scan down the list, you note that almost all of the students that are known to have behavior issues have ended up in your class. Meanwhile, your teaching partner seems to have a class that is much easier to teach with less potential behavior issues.

Your initial reality might be that the administration is being unfair and has made these classes to punish you. However, if you are able to view other realities that might influence their decision, your reality might change.

Positive Reality #1:

You might take it as a compliment. It might be a sign that they respect your classroom management skills and the manner in which you handle students who struggle with self regulation.

Positive Reality #2:

You might believe that you received these students because of your ability to connect with them and be a positive role model that they need.

Positive Reality #3:

You might see that it is an opportunity to develop your classroom management skills and to make a greater impact on the overall school culture.

Being open to other realities in which happiness and success appear possible will increase the likelihood of finding paths in education that are fulfilling and enjoyable.

Turning Positive Realities into Beliefs

Let's revisit the belief statements at the beginning of this chapter. Now think of the impact it would have on our career if we could see positive realities for each statement.

Belief Statement	Considering Positive Realities
I believe that all students can learn.	How would this change your approach for working with students who struggle?
I believe that I have the ability to impact every student's life that I teach.	How would this motivate you to work harder, knowing that you could be that key person in a student's life?

I believe that I can be a leader in my school and/or district.	How would this help you to make positive changes that you feel are needed in your school and/or district?
I believe that change in education starts with me.	How would this impact your motivation to initiate change and to make a difference?
I believe that I can be happy throughout my entire career as a teacher.	How would this push you to find new ways to find your passions as an educator?
I believe that teaching is the best job for me.	How would this empower you to keep growing and working hard without regret?

INSIDE OUT APPROACH

In one of the most popular TED talks of all time, How Great Leaders Inspire Others, Simon Sinek poses the questions, "What is your purpose? What's your cause? What's your belief? Why do you get out of bed in the morning?" He implores us to start with our Why if we want to make a true impact.[15]

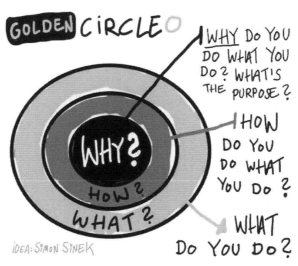

achers who are able to find happiness in education throughout their careers are masters of not only knowing their WHY, but maintaining focus on it. They are not defined by what they do, but WHY they do it.

In his talk, he describes this as the Golden Circle. He states that great leaders and people who find great success take an inside out approach. They start with their WHY at the core of who they are. This WHY drives how they do it and what it is they do!

This is a great way to approach teaching. For instance, if WHY you teach is to positively change as many lives as you can, think of how that will affect how you do your job and what you do in the classroom. It is so important as teachers that we never forget WHY we became teachers. This is what will help us endure the tougher years and will lead us down a path of contentment and fulfillment.

A REASON FOR BEING

In Japan, they have a similar approach to knowing your WHY; it is called Ikigai, meaning 'reason for being.' Part of this culture is the belief that it is essential we find our life's purpose and put it at the center of what we do. It is an intersection of where our passion, mission, profession, and vocation all meet. [16]

IKIGAI
A JANPANESE CONCEPT MEANING 'A REASON FOR BEING

SOURCE: BODETREE, ADAPTED FROM FRANCESC MIRALLES

Ikigai can be a reality for many teachers. By just being a teacher, you are halfway there. You are doing something that the world needs and you are getting paid for it! If you can find a way to be good at it and love it, then you have found your reason for being and this will bring you great happiness.

An interesting fact about Ikigai is that its origin came from the longest living people in the world, the Okinawans- a place in which many men and women live to be over 100 years old. [17] Another interesting fact is that it is the birthplace of Karate! [18]

The key behind both the Golden Circle and the Ikigai philosophy is that it all starts with you believing that what you do is meaningful and that you have the power to make a difference.

It is your beliefs that will lay the groundwork for your entire career in education. These beliefs will control the realities that you manifest, the decisions that you make, and ultimately, the impact you will have. They will be the greatest contributor to your happiness as an educator.

1. In the box provided, make a list of reasons why you became
    an educator.

2. From this list, try to write one powerful sentence that sums
    up the reason that you teach.

    _____

    _____

    _____

3. Now, condense this sentence into your teaching mantra.
    Try to make a phrase consisting of several words. Once you
    get it, write it in the box below.

4. Write this mantra on your day book, in your classroom or
    anywhere you will see it daily to help you stay focused on the
    reason you became a teacher.

Working Towards Happiness

"Happiness is not something ready made.
It comes from your own actions."
— *Dalai Lama XIV*

Happiness, like all things meaningful, requires work. Although it feels like it should occur naturally, it does not. Our brains are not wired to be happy- we have to train them to be happy.

As a busy teacher, the last thing you probably wanted to read was that you have more work to do. However, working towards being happier does not feel like work, it feels amazing. It is a shift in thinking that, in the end, will make life feel easier and more enjoyable.

Simon Sinek said, "Working hard for something we don't care about is called stress. Working hard for something we love is called passion." [19]

One of our top priorities as teachers needs to be that we maintain our passion for teaching. Not only will this love transcend into the classroom and change lives, but it will also help us endure many of the pressures that exist in education. It will allow us to see all of the great aspects and opportunities that come with being an educator.

Diagnose Your Happiness

The machine that optometrists use to test individual lenses on each eye is called a phoropter. The patient looks through this machine at an eye chart as the doctor changes lenses and makes other adjustments. Each time an adjustment is made, the doctor will ask, "Better or Worse?" Eventually, through trial and error and patient feedback, the doctor will find the right lenses to correct the visual impairment.

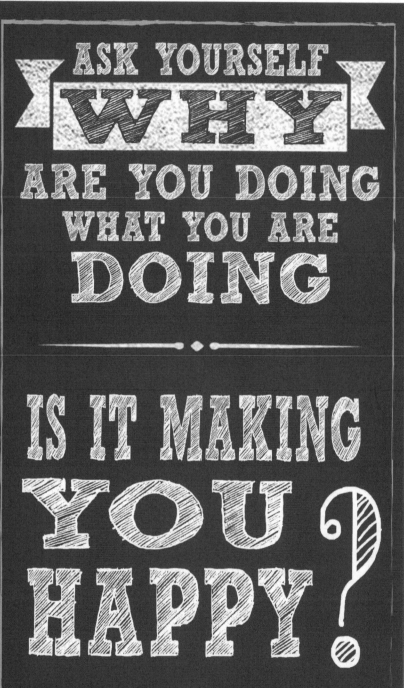

The process of finding happiness works in a very similar way to this machine. To be happy, we need to make sure that we see the world through lenses that give us the best view. As life changes, we need to make the necessary adjustments and constantly ask ourselves, better or worse?

Reflection is such an important aspect of finding and maintaining happiness. Often, we are so busy working, we do not ask ourselves if what we are doing is leading us to a desirable outcome. Without this constant reflection, we begin to lose sight of our end goals, beliefs and our WHY.

Think of how many people do not know their vision is bad until they wear glasses for the first time. For years and years, they saw the world for less than it really was and never realized it. Every day this skewed vision negatively affected their enjoyment, appreciation, and quality of life. It was not until they recognized their impaired vision that they could change it.

Educators can fall into the same trap as people who need glasses and do not know it. Slowly over time, they can begin to lose focus and appreciation for the many great aspects of their jobs. The optimistic lens with which they entered the profession can slowly shift to a view from a more pessimistic lens.

Unfortunately, we do not get a card in the mail every year that reminds us to book our yearly happiness check-up. It is up to us to constantly check in and gauge our level of enjoyment. The more in tune we are, the more likely we are to make the necessary adjustments.

Happiness Prescription

If you have ever had an eye exam, you will remember the optometrist switching through many lenses, trying to find the combination that works best for you. In the end, the prescription that you receive is very specific to your vision.

Finding and maintaining happiness is the same. There is not a magic formula that suits everyone. Each journey is unique. The key is to look for opportunities that will allow you to dial into finding more joy one adjustment at a time. Eventually, you will find a way of living that works for you and allows you to be truly fulfilled.

When taking an eye test, the optometrist starts with a series of standard lenses. As the exam progresses, they begin to fine tune these lenses carefully. This book is going to take a very similar approach. This chapter will outline the five standard habits that have been proven to have the most significant effect on overall subjective well-being.

The remainder of the book will focus on the finer adjustments that exist within the teaching profession. It will be up to you to find the combination that suits you best.

1) Mindfulness

Mindfulness is being present in the moment and experiencing life as it occurs. This sounds like it would be easy to do; however, a recent study showed that we spend 47% of our time awake thinking of something that we are not doing. [20]

The best analogy that I have read regarding this lack of ability to live in the moment was in the book 10% Happier by Dan Harris. He points out that often while eating, we are in search of our next mouthful of food as soon as the fork leaves our mouth. [21] By eating mindlessly like this, we do not get the full enjoyment out of our meal. The same is true of life.

To get the most out of our lives and to increase our levels of contentment, we need to work on living more in the moment. Whether this is stopping to take a deep breath with our students or delving into deep meditation, we need to invest energy into staying present.

2) Exercise

The connection between exercise and health is very well understood and documented. Often our decision to exercise derives from our desire to improve our physical condition, such as body weight, muscle mass, cardiovascular fitness, etc.

We must also respect the impact of exercise in relation to our emotional well-being. Studies have even shown that exercise can be as or more effective than medication in managing depression and anxiety.[22] For instance, the Duke SMILE (Standard Medical Intervention versus Long-term Exercise) study found that exercise and standard antidepressant treatments were equally effective. In addition, it also found that "participants who reported engaging in regular exercise during the follow-up period were more than 50% less likely to be depressed at their 10-month assessment compared to non-exercisers." [23]

It sounds counterintuitive, but expending energy through exercise actually creates more energy. For instance, prior to writing this book, I was struggling with constant fatigue. When I decided to embark on writing, I knew I needed to make some changes to my lifestyle that would enable me to write once my children were sleeping.

Ironically, I found the answer was exercising first, then writing. By getting the blood, oxygen, nutrients, and endorphins flowing throughout my body, it gave me the second wind I needed to do something that I love to do. I began to sleep better, feel better, and developed a more positive attitude throughout the entire day.

3) Detach From Work

As educators, we feel that there is always something we should be doing. We could easily put in 12 hours every day and still have more to do. However, this is not what will be good for us or our students in the long run.

It is essential that, as educators, we carve out time daily to detach from our work. The research shows that moderate-level detachment improves overall life satisfaction, ability to handle stress, reduces irritability and improves overall job performance.[24]

Teacher burnout is a reality for many teachers who are unable to detach from their work. That is why we must schedule time each day to do something that does not relate to work. Something that is a complete disconnect that you enjoy doing.

Finding that appropriate balance can be very challenging for teachers, but is a crucial aspect of maintaining one's long term motivation and joy in the profession.

4) Gratitude

Practicing gratitude is an extremely important habit for teachers to develop. There is a lot to be grateful for in education; however, it is easy to let the pressures and struggles take over. Like happiness, gratitude is something that can be worked on and altered.

More research and focus is now being directed toward gratitude as a means of achieving optimal health and life satisfaction. One of the leading researchers on gratitude, Robert Emmons, has proven positive correlations to improvements in psychological, physical, and social well-being.

In his studies, practicing gratitude led to participants having more energy, alertness, and enthusiasm at work. As well, they sleep better, have lower blood pressure, and participate in exercise more often. These participants also reported feeling less isolated, as they became more outgoing and altruistic.[25]

Incorporating gratitude into day-to-day teaching will have a positive effect on both the teacher and their students. There are many opportunities in education to practice gratitude and reshape the way we see our profession.

5) Relationships

George Couros said it best when he said, "The three most important words in education are Relationships, Relationships, Relationships."[26]

He could not be more right. Teaching is all about fostering relationships. How well we do this will have a major impact on our classroom management, student success, professional growth and leadership as educators, and our overall job fulfillment.

Our relationships with our students, colleagues, and administration are pivotal to our success and happiness. We must make caring, recognizing, appreciating and respecting those we interact with daily a focus in our lives. Without these relationships, there is little joy.

Taking Control of Your 40%

How happy we are comes down to how well we manage the 40% of our happiness that we have control over. This is true in life and in education. It is our daily thoughts, routines, interactions, and beliefs that will mold us into the person and the teacher we want to be.

I want to be clear that I am not a psychologist. I am a teacher - a teacher who has struggled with being happy in the profession. It was not until I realized that I had control of my own emotional well-being that everything started to change.

The habits promoted to improve happiness by experts in the field of positive psychology really work. Through my personal experiences and conversations with many educators, I believe that everyone is on their own journey to find contentment in the profession. The educators who are successful are the ones that seize the many opportunities that are presented throughout their careers.

The rest of this book is about opportunities for happiness in education. The hope is that the strategies, stories, insights, and realizations of other educators will accelerate your own journey toward finding deep passion and happiness in the classroom.

PART ONE:

Under each of the Happiness Habits, draw a dot representing the amount of deliberate attention you invest towards making these a priority in your life.

MINDFULNESS

Low   High

EXERCISE

Low   High

DETACH FROM WORK

Low   High

EXPERIENCING FLOW

Low   High

DEVELOPING STRONG RELATIONSHIPS

Low   High

PART TWO: Reflection

The above self reflection tool will give you an idea of habits that you may want to explore more. Keep this in mind as you read the rest of the book. There will be many profession-embedded ideas that will hopefully allow you to include more of these habits in your teaching.

PART TWO: STRIVE

STUDENTS:
Deep Connections

"When educating the minds of our youth, we must not forget to educate their hearts."
- Dalai Lama

The greatest opportunity for happiness in education sits right in front of us every day. They are hard to ignore and they are the reason we became teachers. Without them, there is no us. In many ways, students are our Ikigai. They sit at the center of everything that we do, and they give us a deep purpose in our professional lives.

Beyond giving us a purpose, students also provide us with the opportunity to develop meaningful and lasting relationships. By taking the time to get to know our students at a deeper level, we are creating the conditions for many great outcomes to occur. These relationships that were developed in the classroom can lead to many more moments of joy throughout the lives of both the student and the teacher.

We must strive to always make students our number one priority when we come to work each day. The better we are at focusing on them, the more likely we are to find happiness and fulfillment in education.

Belief and Mindset

Building great relationships with students starts with the belief that everyone in our class is special and deserves to be loved and cared for. We must believe that they all have greatness in them, and that we could be the person to help them realize it.

ALWAYS TRY TO FIND
THE GOOD
IN EACH STUDENT

ESPECIALLY
WHEN THEY ARE
STRUGGLING

Transforming these beliefs into action starts with the development of a positive mindset toward each student. We must always look to find the good in them. Whether it be a talent, personality trait, or a skill, it is up to us to recognize and celebrate it. The more we make getting to know them a priority, the more likely we are to discover their true potential.

It is easy to be positive when things are going good, and essential to be positive when things are going poorly. Students need us the most when they are struggling. They need our help to turn the corner and get back on track. Learning how to maintain a positive mindset through adversity will significantly help us build strong relationships with the students who need us the most.

Look at each student like a puzzle that you know has a solution. Take the time to analyze each piece carefully, stay positive, be patient, and look for connections that will lead you closer to solving them.

STUDENT HYPER-FOCUS

The happiest teachers whom I have had the pleasure of meeting do not just focus on their students — they hyper-focus on their students. It is almost like these teachers wear blinders similar to those you see in horse races. They have learned how to block out a lot of the other distractions that are prevalent in education so they can invest more into their students.

Once I asked Wendy, the spunky redhead who inspired me to find more enjoyment in education, how she was able to navigate all of the stresses that tend to weigh other teachers down. Her response was simple, "I just focus more on my students, they are what I love most about education, so I focus on them the most. That is what makes me happy."

FROM DAY ONE

One of the best realizations I had as a teacher occurred spontaneously on the first day of school during my introductory address to the class- I was not prepared for it. Looking into a whole new set of faces that I knew only through quick encounters in the halls, I realized that these unknown faces would, in ten months, mean as much to me as the students who used to sit in those desks.

Here is the embarrassing part. As I explained this to my new class, my eyes completely welled up and I choked up, "I have come to the realization that I will love you by the end of the year, and I want you to know that everything that I do from today on will be done out of love and your best interest."

They were shocked. Can you imagine your macho 250lb. teacher crying on the first day of school and confessing his love to you? It was quite the moment and one that set the tone for an amazing year. Each year since, I start my class explaining to my students this realization because I think it is crucial they know from day one how much I care about them and how invested I am in their lives.

Happy to Know You

There is a great deal of happiness to be found in getting to know our students beyond their student records and academic performance. They are fascinating young people who can teach us as much as we can teach them if we are willing to learn.

Teachers who find the most fulfillment are the ones that are able to create strong connections with their students. These connections are developed through getting to know each other at a deeper level. It is not enough to leave these connections to chance, we need to find ways to create connections that we can build on throughout the year.

Why wait? Invest the first couple of days planning activities and assignments that will give you valuable insight into who they are and what they like. The quicker we are able to get a read on a student, the quicker we can begin the process of developing a stronger connection.

Scratching the Surface

The first few days of school can be intense for both students and the teacher. It is a great idea to incorporate ice breakers throughout the day to help ease tension and to start the process of building community. Speaking from experience, we must select these activities carefully. Ice breakers can very quickly backfire or can often lead to meaningless banter.

When selecting the first icebreaker of the year, we must always consider the initial comfort level of our class and what information we are asking them to divulge publicly. Choose an activity that does not involve students taking major social risks where they are put on the spot or asked to do something silly that might embarrass them.

The goal of these activities is to help everyone get to know each other better. Try to choose activities that will give you insight and help form connections between everyone in the room. Here are some examples of great icebreakers that students will love and that will quickly teach you a lot about them as individuals and as a group.

Pick One:

Divide the room in half with all students on one side. Explain to them that you will be giving them two choices and they have to 'Pick One' by moving to the side of the room delegated. Explain to them that you must go to one side or the other. Start off with simple questions that everyone will be comfortable answering, such as;

- Sweet or salty?
- Summer or winter?
- Disneyland or private beach?

As the game progresses, intermix questions that give you deeper insight into who they are. Think through what information you want to gain from this activity ahead of time and build it into the questions you ask. Encourage students to look at who is on their side each time to promote familiarity among them. Most importantly, participate in this activity with them. It is as much about them getting to know you, as it is you getting to know them.

Quick Chats:

Set up the room so that there is an inner and outer circle of students facing each other. Ensure that each student is paired up with another student face to face. Set a timer and provide a question that will spark a short discussion between the partners. Have the outer group rotate one space in the same direction, answering a different question each time. This is a great way to encourage one-to-one conversations. Here are some key things to remember when setting up this type of activity:

- You must get involved. Set it up so that you are one of the participants. This way, you get an opportunity to learn and connect with different students in your class.

- Use technology (i.e., slideshow) to facilitate the questions and timing. This will allow you to focus on learning about students, not pressing start and cueing up the next question.

- Ask questions that will promote conversation and give you an avenue to get to know them better, such as:
    - What aspect of school do you enjoy the most?
    - What was your best experience last year at school?
    - What would you change about school if you had the power?

- Do not feel that everyone needs to talk to everyone. Gauge when the activity begins to lose steam and come back to it another time.

Dotmocracy:

Around the room, post a series of papers with different aspects of what they might be looking most forward to this school year. For instance;

- New teachers
- Extracurriculars
- Class trips
- Classroom/physical space
- Classmates
- Timetable/subjects
- Projects
- Homework

Ask them if you are missing anything; if so, create and post it. Now give them a set number of dots or stickers (I usually do around 30 each). Allow them to place the stickers on the aspects of the year that they are most excited about. How they disperse these stickers will give you a great insight into who they are as students. At the end, have a discussion and ask students to volunteer where and why they invested their dots where they did. As an extension, use a different color sticker at the end of the year to see what they ended up enjoying the most. It is a fun way to reflect on the year.

After completing an icebreaker activity like the ones mentioned above, take time to reflect and make quick notes on what you learned about each particular student and/or the group as a whole. Use these initial observations to create connections and to plan your approach for upcoming lessons.

And the Survey Says...

My first assignment of the year was one of the most meaningful. It was a basic set of questions that I created to get to know my students better. There were approximately 12 questions ranging from favorite TV show to least favorite subject in school. It might seem like a pretty standard assignment, but for me, it started the process of getting to know them and planning out a great year for them.

When I read each of these questionnaires, I made a note of things that I would use throughout the entire year to connect to the students. For instance, if a student had difficulty opening up or engaging in a specific class, I would refer to my notes to see what sparked their interest. The next lesson, I would try to use a clip from their favorite movie or try to integrate something they had written down on their sheet into the lesson. The students appreciated my attempt to make learning interesting for them and that I was taking the time to get to know them.

After a graduation ceremony, one of my former students approached me and said, "I knew you cared about me because you used to always pretend that you liked horses. It meant a lot to me that you cared enough to try." I only knew she liked horses so much because of the form she filled out on the first day.

To modernize this activity, use online survey tools such as Google Forms or Survey Monkey. Students will enjoy the infusion of technology and you will have their responses collated and easy to access throughout the year.

The surveys themselves have little value unless you use them in a way that is meaningful. Just as feedback forms are meaningless unless you use them to refine what you are doing. Revisiting these surveys throughout the year is a great tactic when looking to connect with elusive students!

TIP OF THE ICEBERG

By the end of the first week, you should have some understanding of the class that sits in front of you. You might already have made some great connections, but don't stop there. Make it your mission to keep learning about your students all year long. The deeper this knowledge, the greater the likelihood of happiness for everyone involved.

Many of these relationships will develop naturally over time if you continually show interest. However, there are different ways to embed getting to know your students better throughout the year that will ensure these connections continue to deepen. Here are a couple ideas to get you started!

PASSION PORTFOLIOS

One keepsake that I still have from my elementary days is my journal. Back then, the teacher would put a prompt on the board, and we would do our best to respond. So naturally, when I became a teacher, I did the same. Overall, I think it had value, but I feel that it could have been more meaningful.

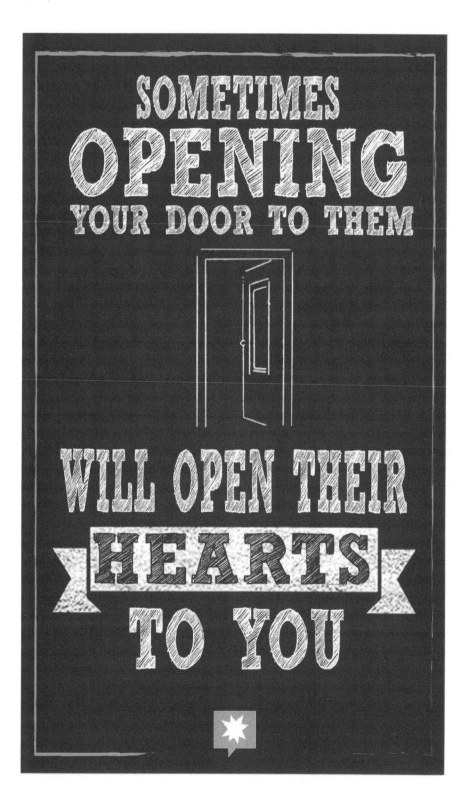

Enter the idea of Passion Portfolios. Imagine that this time was invested in doing something that I truly loved or wanted to explore. I could have written song lyrics, created a comic book, drew buildings to scale, designed a video game or invented something amazing. How much cooler would that have been?

I love the idea of students' Passion Portfolios looking different. Some might decide to use a pad of graph paper, a sketchbook, or a self decorated journal. Allow them to be creative, to create something that is unique and represents them.

On an awesome side note, my mother-in-law went to high school with James Cameron, the famous filmmaker. She remembers him drawing the characters from Avatar on his math books decades before anyone knew who he was. I can only imagine how cool his Passion Portfolio would have looked and the many insights it would have given his teachers into this very creative and talented mind.

I think the power in Passion Portfolios is two-fold. Firstly, I think it is great to promote choice and exploring passions over a longer duration of time. This way students can continue to build on a passion they have or look to discover passions they never knew existed. Secondly, I think it is a great tool to get to know students on a deeper level. Watching them excel at their natural talent or helping them struggle to find something that interests them, creates many opportunities for conversations that are meaningful to them.

Combining Passion Portfolios with regular feedback sessions will give you an amazing view into who that student is, and it will present you with many opportunities to enrich your connection. For the student, these portfolios could lead them to develop the signature skill that brings them much delight. It might also increase their enjoyment by allowing them to experience the feeling of flow throughout each day.

Passion Portfolios could also be an amazing precursor to Genius Hour type projects. These portfolios will provide students time to work through their ideas, find their passion, and develop their genius. Too often, we spring these types of projects on students with not enough time to truly develop or connect with a passion.

Open Invites

The best way to really get to know your students is to make yourself available. Teaching can be very hectic at times, and there are always thousands of things that you could be doing. However, few things will impact your happiness more than getting to know your students better.

I think it is key to have an open-door policy with students. They should know that you are there for them when they need you. Often, we tell students this at the beginning of the year and assume that they just drop in as needed. However, students are very perceptive. They see how busy you are on breaks, dealing with issues, photocopying, setting up lessons, meeting with administration, etc. Some students are too polite or too shy to just walk in and expect your attention. They will feel like they need to have a major concern or issue to monopolize your time.

This is where Open Invites come into play. On those days that you have extra time, you need a boost, or you just want something to take you away from marking, offer up an open invitation for students to drop in. Whether you announce it to the class or post an Open Invite sign on the door, make it known that you would like to get to know them better.

It will surprise you who will show up and how much you will learn about students in this relatively short period. Try to find ways to make this time fun and meaningful. Personally, I found that it was always less awkward socializing with students when we were engaged in an activity of some sort. If you feel the same, suggest going for walks, playing cards, or participating in other activities that you enjoy.

Do not perceive these open invites as extra work or something you must do. You need to believe in the value of these informal meetings. They should be something that you look forward to and enjoy. It is a great way to take a break, while at the same time doing something fun and meaningful.

Setting the Scene

Just as there are many opportunities to experience happiness every day, there are many opportunities to make connections with students every day. The key is to not only search for those opportunities, but to create situations for them to occur.

Doing the activities above will not guarantee that you will build deep and meaningful connections, but it will help set the scene for that to occur. Here are some other ideas that will help to build strong and meaningful relationships with students.

Make Them Feel Special

Try to find a unique angle with each student. For instance, it might be an ongoing joke, nickname, or fancy handshake. Be on the lookout for your opportunity to find that thing that makes them feel special.

Greet Them Daily

One simple way to let your students know you care and to build connections is to greet them individually before they enter the classroom. A recent study showed that when students were welcomed at the door, academic engagement increased by 20%, and disruptive behavior dropped by 9%. [27] It is a great way to start off each day and to build relationships.

Show Up Just For Them

Nothing means more to a student when a teacher shows up to an event that is special to them. Whether that is a sporting event, concert, or graduation, be there if you can. It is always great seeing them in their element, and it will mean the world to them that you showed up.

Recognize Them Often

Let them know that you are aware of the great things that they are doing. Whether it be a quick comment on their work, sticky note on their desk, or a card, take the time to recognize them and make them feel special.

Create Situations for Relationships to Blossom

Often, breakthrough moments getting to know students better happen outside of instructional time. I love the idea of planning a class trip at the beginning of the year. Many times, these trips give both teachers and students an opportunity to get to know each other better. Creating opportunities like this at the beginning of the year gives you time to further develop the relationships.

One Conversation at a Time

Relationships take time to build. Every interaction we have with students is meaningful and will contribute to the quality of the relationship that is developed. To earn their love and respect, we must be patient and consistent in our interactions with them. We need to treat them how we would like to be treated. Here are some tips when connecting with students daily:

- Be present. Give them your undivided attention.
- Listen more than you speak.
- Ask questions that show you care.

- Share information about yourself.
- Show enjoyment (laugh, joke, smile…).
- Be there when they are struggling.
- Give great advice.
- Offer ongoing support.

Most Importantly, Care About Them

More than anything, students need an adult in their lives who authentically cares about them. They need someone who enjoys them and wants to spend time getting to know them. They need someone they know will be there for them. They need someone they can trust and depend on. Every student needs someone special in their lives.

A study by Harvard's Center on the Developing Child released this quote, "Every child who winds up doing well has had at least one stable and committed relationship with a supportive adult." [28]

Be that person for them. There is so much to gain if you can. An investment in them is an investment in happiness for both of you.

PART ONE: Graphing

The Happiest Teachers are extra focused on their students, and less focused on the negative aspects of the profession. On the circle graph below, estimate where your energy goes.

Divide this circle graph into 2 sections by drawing one more line.

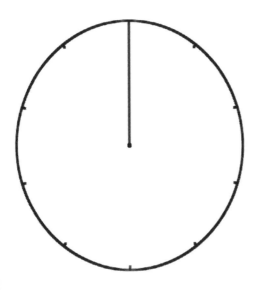

Label one section that represents the amount of your energy that focuses on students.

Divide up the remaining section of the circle graph to indicate where the rest of your energy is focused (ie. PD, planning, parents, leadership, staff drama, ect.).

PART TWO: Reflection

1. Are you happy with the amount of your energy that is focused on students? If not, why?

2. What negative aspects of education are taking your focus away from students? Which of these do you have control over? Which of these do you need to focus less on?

3. What can you do to make sure more of your energy is focused on making connections with your students?

STUDENTS:
THOSE WHO NEED US THE MOST

*"The children who need love the most will
always ask for it in the most unloving ways."*
— *Russell Barkley*

Every student deserves a quality education, but that does not mean they require an equal amount of effort and focus from their teachers. Many students will flow seamlessly through the education system and will move on to great things regardless of the teachers they cross. They are the leaders, helpers, and the students you can depend on throughout the day. These students already know how to be successful and understand the importance of hard work. However, the students you least expect will change your life and help you develop into the teacher you have always dreamt of becoming.

We have all seen the movies in which a coach or a teacher has changed the lives of their players or students, where the longshot triumphs in the end due to the intervention of key individuals. Education offers you the opportunity to be that life-altering figure many times and for many students.

One of the keys to happiness and fulfillment in teaching is to search out the students who are struggling the most in your classroom. They offer the best win-win situation possible. These students find a teacher who cares for them, advocates for them, guides them, cheers them on, and makes them a priority, maybe for the first time in their lives. For a teacher, these students provide challenges, inspiration, job satisfaction, and a greater purpose in your role as an educator.

Be consciously aware each day of the impact you could potentially have on these students' lives. They will be easy to disregard or remove from the classroom. Make a commitment to be there for them over the long term, to be willing to fail daily, and to continue to advocate for these students as long as you have the opportunity. They will test you. Until they know how much you care, they won't care. These students will be a lot of work, but witnessing the payoff is priceless.

It Is Possible

I was fortunate to have an experience early in my career that shaped my appreciation for struggling students. This student was the tallest boy in my grade seven class and the most disengaged. Being new to teaching, I was struggling to keep up with the daily workload and had found it easier to avoid trying to encourage his love for learning. I would simply give him a short lecture and call home when he acted up or failed to complete his homework. He was very apathetic for the most part and did not seem to care about anything. As the school year progressed, it seemed impossible to get an assignment or even a word from him in class.

I remember the day clearly when I pulled him aside after school and told him that I was going to call his parents yet again. To my shock, he exploded in anger and told me that I was ruining his life and that every time I called, his home life got worse and worse. He then stormed off. Confused by the situation, I did not call home and stewed over it all night. I decided I was going to try something different.

I watched him closely throughout the next day and noticed something unusual. He would twirl his pencil repeatedly, and his lips would move each time. Then I realized that he was so bored that he was counting the number of times he was twirling it. Not the most flattering realization of my career. At the end of the day, I asked him to meet me again. He confirmed that he was counting the twirls because in his words, "It was so boring."

I could not imagine how long a day would feel if you were counting each second. So, I thought about it and decided to make him a deal that changed everything. I created a list of five things that he needed to do the following day to get out of me calling home. The list went as follows:

1. Stand and sit up straight when in the classroom.
2. Focus on the lesson.
3. Participate each time you know the answer.
4. Try the homework.
5. Meet me after school the following day, and be prepared to answer several questions regarding your day.

His response was, "Is that all?" He agreed. Neither of us knew the impact this would have.

I vividly remember him walking in the next morning, reluctantly correcting his posture when I looked at him. With each lesson, I made sure he knew I was tracking his focus. I made a point of starting the lesson with easier questions to see if he would commit to answering and he did. When it came time to do the in-class work, he actually started to work on it, which surprised me. This routine went on throughout the day, and he showed up after school, with the immediate question, "So am I off the hook now?"

I reminded him of his final commitment to answer several questions, and he hesitantly slid down into a seat. Below is the conversation that changed everything for us.

"How was today?" I asked.

"Ok."

"Be more specific."

"I don't know. What do you want me to say?" he said abruptly.

"Well, was it better or worse than yesterday?" I probed.

"I don't know," he said and shrugged me off again.

I continued with my next question, "Did you learn anything you did not know?"

Lighting up just slightly, he said, "Well, I have never heard of that liquid thing you were talking about in science. It was cool, I guess."

"So, would you say it was more or less interesting than yesterday?"

"More, I guess," he answered with less hesitancy.

So, I continued, "How was the homework today?"

Quickly he blurted out, "Easy. I finished it in class. It was a joke."

"And, did today go by slower or quicker than yesterday?"

"Quicker," he admitted after thinking about it.

"Now I am going to ask you again, was today better than yesterday, yes or no?"

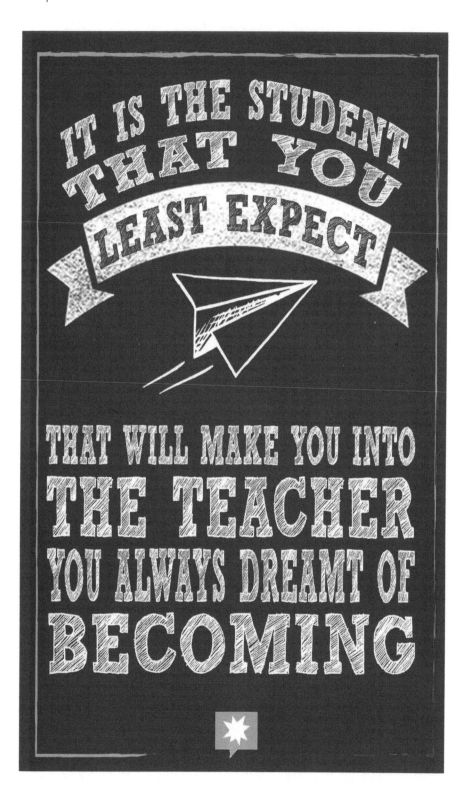

With a slight pause, he answered, "Yes, I guess it was better."

"And when you leave, if I was to call home…?"

Exploding with anger, he raised his voice, "We had a deal! The deal was no more phone calls home…"

"Let me finish," I interrupted. "If I called home and tell them how great of a day you had today, what would happen?"

With his eyes welling up with tears, he responded, "I don't know."

"Well, let's see what happens. The last thing that I want you to think about is this. If today was better than yesterday, went by quicker and was more interesting, why don't you just do this every day and see what happens."

That night I did call home, and the parents were shocked to get a call of this positive nature. They went out to dinner to celebrate. From that day forward, he followed the suggestions I had given him. So much so that I had to limit the number of questions he was able to answer throughout the day. He quickly gained the respect of his peers and became an inspiration in our classroom.

I had the privilege of teaching him again in his grade eight year, and he was, for lack of a better term, unstoppable. I remember collecting a science test from him, and on the top of his page, he had written in bold letters that he "aced it," and he had.

At graduation that year, he received several awards. One of them was the Science Award with a 93% average. At the end of the night ,he smiled at me and said, "Thanks for speeding up school for me." I replied, "Thanks for making my year for me."

Four years later, I attended his high school graduation. Grown into a man, he wore his graduation gown draped with a ribbon that signified he had achieved an over 80% average throughout high school. When he proudly walked across that stage, they announced that he would be attending college to become an electrical engineer. It was one of the most inspiring and unforgettable moments of my life.

I feel a deep sense of gratitude towards this student as my experience with him has contributed to many other moments I cherish as a teacher. He taught me that it is possible to reach students who do not seem interested in learning or making changes that will enable them to be more successful in the future. He taught me that there is a great deal of untapped potential in students who struggle the most. And most importantly, he taught me that I had the ability to reach those students. This became a motivating factor for me as an educator and a true source of happiness.

DIFFERENT APPROACH

We must believe that we have the ability to help any student. Without this belief, we will miss helping the ones who need us the most. Do your best to disregard other educators if they try to convince you that a student cannot be helped. Believe that you can and keep trying until the last day of school.

It is a good idea to research the approaches that other teachers have used to help support this type of student. This will probably give you a quick insight into what does not work. From there, you can begin to implement new and unconventional ways of making the necessary connection you will need to be successful.

It is the quality of the relationship that you have with a student, that will determine the amount of impact that is possible. It will be a lot harder to establish relationships with a student who has deep issues. Be realistic with regards to your expectations and your timeline. Do not expect icebreakers and surveys to be enough to help you create this connection, you will need to go much deeper.

CREATE A PROFILE

The more you know about a student, the more likely you are to be able to connect with them. It is key to do your homework on a student that needs your help. Read their student file, talk to other teachers and, if possible, get to know their family. This will give you a good base to determine when they started to struggle and potentially why.

Combine what you have learned about the student with what you observe daily. Continually add to their profile and work on developing a deeper understanding of who they are. Here are some key areas to pay close attention to:

- How they interact with their peers?
- Which student, if any, are they drawn to? Why?
- Which students frustrate them?
- How are they perceived by other students?
- What causes them to shut down or act out?
- What activities frustrate them the most?
- What time of day, week, or year do they struggle the most?

- Where are they confident? Unconfident?
- What skills do they possess that they might not see?
- What will they do if they are given free time?
- What healthy/unhealthy patterns do you observe (sleep, addictions, nutrition, etc.)?
- What, if anything, do they enjoy about school?
- What do they do for recreation outside of school hours?

As your profile develops, be on the lookout for key opportunities that will help make the student's time in your classroom more tolerable. Perhaps it is a seating arrangement that positions them with someone that they might connect with or build in activities to the day that might give them something to look forward to. Try to see these actions as not giving into the student. Instead, view it as trying to get the ball rolling in the right direction.

Filling in the Gaps

As you grow to know more about a struggling student, try to determine where the major gaps in their enjoyment and connections are with school. There are reasons that these students are not invested in their education. It is up to you to try to figure out what is missing and be the first person to provide it for them.

There are common reasons that students tend to really struggle in a classroom setting. Here is a list of gaps that these students are missing and that you might be able to fill:

Trust	Grew up in an environment with adults who were inconsistent. Learned to expect being let down.
Self-Worth	Do not understand their value. This plays a major role in their confidence and ability to interact with others.
Confidence	They are so used to failing (in their mind) that this becomes the expectation from the start.
Learning	Gaps in their learning, lead to their constant struggle and falling behind. Easier to avoid than to catch up.

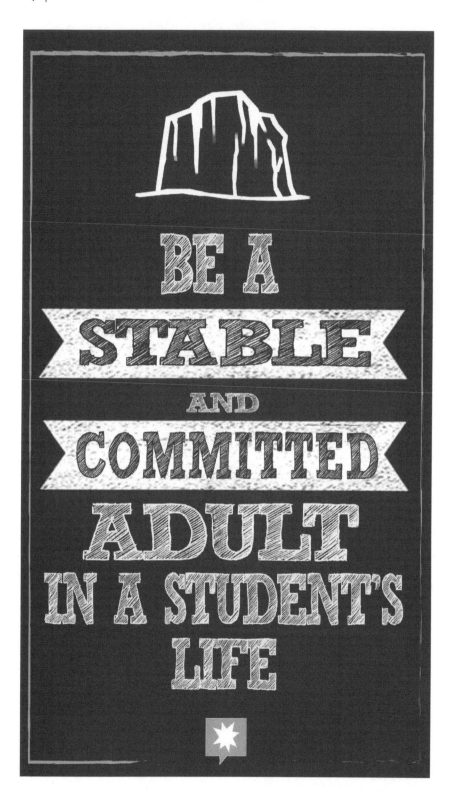

Vision	They do not see the value in learning and education. Very little incentive to try if they do not believe there is a positive outcome waiting.
Fear	They are scared to put themselves out there in case they fail or succeed.
Belief	They do not believe that success is possible. The reality that they have created makes it seem impossible.

Once you have a handle on the major gaps that impact the student's success, you can start to build them up in that area or be that person that helps them see their true potential.

Consistent Authentic Caring

Students who struggle the most need a person in their lives who makes them feel like they are a priority. They need to get the sense that you truly and deeply care about them and their well-being. These students are able to sense if you are being nice to them in order to improve classroom management or because you are intimidated.

The only way to make a student genuinely understand your level of commitment towards them is to demonstrate consistency over a lengthy period of time. These students have most likely had people come into their lives with passion and ambition, and then watched them fade away. Be the one that does not fade away, does not give up, and convinces them that you will be there when they need you.

It is so essential that you are authentic in your intent and your approach. You need to really want to strive to be that person for that student. This needs to be something that you want to do, not that you feel obligated to do. If this is the case, then when it does get frustrating or tiring, you will most likely gravitate to something else that requires your attention.

It is the everyday interactions that will build credibility with these students. Find creative ways to develop opportunities to connect and to make them valuable. Here are some tips on how to gradually build connections with even the toughest to get to know students:

- **Seek Them Out** because chances are, they are not going to pursue you to change their lives. The key is to make this feel natural.

For instance, be visible to them when they arrive at school in the morning, somewhere that might lead to a short conversation. Create an opportunity near the end of the day to check on how their day went or to offer extra support.

- **Be Present** in each conversation that you have with them. Try your best to give them your focus, if they are willing to give you their time. If for whatever reason, there are too many distractions at that moment, offer to set aside more time where you can fully focus.

- **Read Where They Are** and be willing to listen when they need you to listen; be willing to dispense advice when they are looking for advice. Try not to always have an agenda. Let the relationship advance at a pace that is comfortable for them.

- **Smile and Laugh** when it is possible. Creating a bond is all about enjoying each other's company. Make sure you smile when you see them, laugh when something is funny and joke around when the time seems right. Don't always be serious.

- **Be Positive and Supportive.** Build discussions around subjects that are highlighting the good things that are going on. If they are struggling and confide in you, be supportive and help them find a positive point of view or a way to move forward.

- **Show an Interest in Them.** Use the time you have with them to learn more about them. Let them know that you enjoy getting to know them. Do not probe too hard. Allow them to open up as they feel more comfortable.

BUILDING TRUST

Each consecutive day that you invest in getting to know them and supporting them builds trust. With struggling students, this will be a slow process, and one that can be reversed quickly if not careful. Remember that these students are usually emotionally fragile. They may put on a tough front, but deep down, they are struggling and very skeptical. Here are some key areas where trust can be built or broken.

- **Honor Commitments.** It is critical if you say you are going to do something with them or for them, that you do it. Each commitment you keep shows that you are making them a priority and that you are someone they can trust.

- **Stand Up for Them.** Take a special interest in how other people treat this type of student. Defend them when they need defending, and be there to support them when they make mistakes. Be there beside them in good or bad situations.

- **Be Consistent.** These students need someone who is predictable. Part of building trust is knowing what lies ahead. They need to see you as the constant in their lives. Be the person that they can count on every day to support and guide them.

- **Be Fair.** There will probably be times throughout the relationship-building process that you will need to discipline these students. Try to avoid overreacting. Find a solution that holds the student accountable, while at the same time being agreed upon as fair.

- **Share.** To learn more about a student, you must be willing to allow them to learn more about you. Sharing parts of your past allows you to find relatable stories and experiences. It is in these commonalities that camaraderie and trust are built.

BE CREATIVE

The final suggestion is to be creative with your approach to helping them overcome their struggles, negative thoughts, and destructive patterns. Always be on the lookout for opportunities to create situations in which the student can experience success and growth.

This has always been my favorite part of the job. I try to always see students who are struggling as a challenge. This drives me to create situations in which student's natural talents surface. Similar to solving a puzzle or a breakout room, there is a great deal of satisfaction when it happens.

Once I created a Connect Four club specifically because I knew the student I was mentoring at the time would win. He did, and it was awesome. Another time, I videotaped a lip sync music video starring the student that no one liked. Not only was this the highlight of my year, he was selected as a runner up for valedictorian at graduation.

If you want the student to succeed bad enough, you will be willing to go that extra mile for them. They will consume your mind and tap into the creativity that you didn't even know existed. Enjoy this challenge and if you get them, nothing in teaching will be more rewarding.

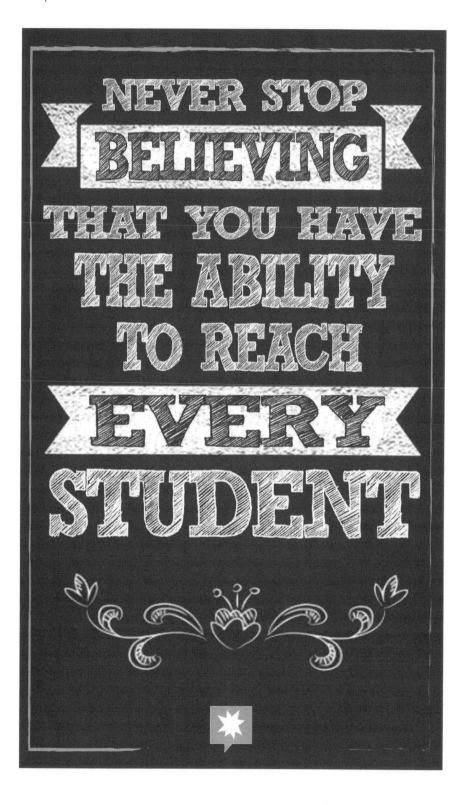

THE BREAKTHROUGH

At some point that will seem totally random to you, a breakthrough might occur. All of a sudden, this student is the one looking for you when they get off the bus or dropping in just to say goodbye. You become perhaps the most important and anticipated part of their day. You have experienced a breakthrough.

The energy that you have invested day in and day out will all seem worth it when you begin to feel like you are making progress. The relationship will start to feel less forced and more natural. It is at this point, you will be able to truly impact this student, and they will begin to impact you.

Even beyond the breakthrough, continue to work hard with these students. Once you have gained their trust and respect, you now play a powerful role in guiding them towards a happier future. Take this role seriously, and you could be the one teacher that they will always credit for changing their lives.

There is so much happiness to be found in helping students who really need it. This is the type of joy that revisits you often and completely fulfills you. Throughout your life, you will never forget their names, their story or that amazing feeling you get when you recall your impact on their life. Be that teacher!

1. In the box provided, write the name(s) of one or two
    students that you feel you have had the greatest impact
    on in your career?

2. Reflect on what you did that helped you make this impact on
    their lives? What did you need to do differently to connect
    with them and help them find success and happiness?

3. In the box provided, write down words that represent the
    emotions you feel when you think about these students that
    your have deeply impacted.

4. In the box provided, write the name of a student who really
    needs you. Commit to being 'that teacher' for them.

TEAM:
Teacher Friends Forever

"You are the average of the top five people
you spend the most time with."
— Jim Rohn

Who do you choose to eat lunch with at work? Who do you call when you need teacher advice? Which teachers on staff do you make an effort to keep in contact with over the summer? Who are your TFFs?

In a global study of over 150 countries, Gallup analyzed the major contributors to well-being. An interesting finding that emerged from the study was that, "30% of respondents who reported having a best friend at work were seven times more likely to be engaged at their jobs than respondents who didn't." [29]

The development of these friendships could very likely be the difference between you being happy in education or not. Some of the most powerful research in the field of positive psychology supports the idea that the quality of our relationships is the most powerful predictor of happiness, health, and longevity. Let's take a look at the research!

The Harvard Study of Adult Development

Over 80 years ago, scientists at Harvard embarked on what is now one of the longest ongoing studies on adult life. The goal of this study was to determine what factors contributed to living a healthy and happy life. They closely analyzed the physical and mental health of 268 sophomores and their offspring throughout their entire lives. Their findings highlighted the importance of nurturing quality relationships.

Robert Waldinger, the Director of the study, admits that they were surprised to discover how our powerful relationships impact our overall health. So much so that they released this very conclusive statement, "Good 'relationships keep us happier and healthier. Period."[30]

THE VERY HAPPY PEOPLE STUDY

What do happy people have in common? This was the question that Martin Seligman, the father of positive psychology, set out to answer by analyzing the Happiest 10% of people that they could find. Of the 222 undergraduates in the study, they discovered there was only one common thread that tied the happiest 10% together — the strength of their social relationships.[31]

Shawn Achor's study on well-being also strongly supported this correlation between relationships and happiness. His empirical study of 1600 Harvard undergraduates concluded that, "social support was a far greater predictor of happiness than any other factor, more than GPA, family income, SAT scores, age, gender or race."[32]

SOCIAL RELATIONSHIPS & MORTALITY RISKS STUDY

Not only does socializing make you happier, it also impacts how long you will live. In a meta-analysis of 148 studies involving 308,849 participants, Julianne Holt-Lunstad and her team were able to determine that the two most powerful predictors of living longer were Social Integration and Close Relationships.[33]

These two predictors towered above lifestyle choices such as exercising, body composition, hypertension, flu vaccination, quitting smoking/drinking, and clean air.

ARE INTROVERTS DOOMED?

Definitely not. However, some research suggests that introverts are generally more likely to report lower levels of happiness relative to extroverts.[34] This is just a generalization and obviously does not apply to everyone. If you consider yourself an introvert and you are very happy, then you might not need to invest in more socialization. If on the other hand, you feel that being an introvert is negatively impacting your happiness, you might find this chapter very useful.

A recent study asked participants to act like an introvert for one week and an extrovert for another week. Then the subjects completed surveys assessing their levels of mood and well-being. The most interesting finding was that introverts had elevated positive moods during their extrovert week, supporting the idea that even introverts can positively benefit from more socialization.[35]

Developing a strong self-awareness of what makes you happy is very important. Sometimes you must go outside of your comfort zone to find more happiness and sometimes there is true happiness in being comfortable and not needing more. Each of us owes it to ourselves to learn what makes us the happiest.

Blue Zones of Happiness

The Blue Zones are the five regions of the world where people live the longest and healthiest lives. Through studying these regions, author Dan Buettner has been able to identify nine factors that contribute to their longevity.[36] The one that pertains most to this chapter is finding the "Right Tribe."

Buettner describes the "Right Tribe" as finding or creating social circles that support healthy behaviors.[37] He also notes that his research shows that, "The happiest people in the world spend a whopping five to six hours a day socializing face-to-face with people they like and with whom they can have meaningful conversations."[38] Not only is this essential to a long and happy life, but also a long and happy teaching career.

Finding the Right Team

Just because we know something is important does not mean it is easy to accomplish. Surrounding yourself with the right team in education takes time, effort, and perseverance. We must make it a priority not only to nurture friendships at work, but also to seek out the type of friends who will contribute greatly to our success and enjoyment as educators.

A good starting point is taking the time to analyze the different personalities that you work with each day. Pay close attention to those educators who:

- Handle stress effectively.
- Have fun at work.
- Enjoy socializing with both students and staff.
- Find joy in teaching.
- Make those around them better.
- Are trustworthy and honest.
- Are encouraging to others.

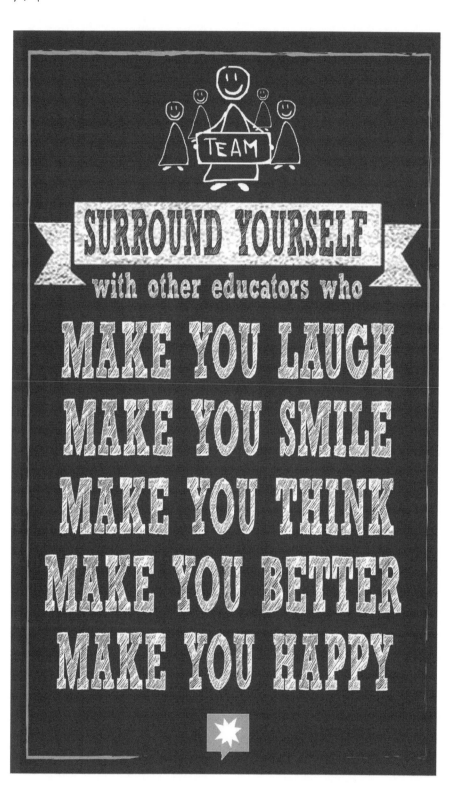

Now, using these characteristics and others that you might have added, reflect on how others on staff would see you. If another teacher on your staff read this chapter, would you stand out to them as someone that could have a positive impact on their overall happiness and experience at work and beyond.

If the answer is yes, then continue to do what you are doing. If your answer is no, then try to make the necessary changes that will draw the right people to you. It is not just enough to find a great team, you must also work on attracting the right team to you.

One Caution

When surrounding yourself with a positive team be cautious of accentuating cliques and divides in the staff. It is easy to isolate yourself from people who are not as positive as we would like them to be. However, this is not going to have a positive impact on the staff, students, or the culture in the building.

Be open to building relationships with them. Just like those students who need us the most, there are educators on staff who struggle and need support. Helping others on staff to find more joy at work can be very fulfilling and impactful. Not only that, you may uncover a TFF that you would have missed!

INVEST IN YOURSELF

The Law of Attraction states that energy flows where attention goes.[39] To draw the right people into our circle, we must focus our energy on becoming better at what we do and who we are. If we are able to do that, then we will naturally increase our chances of developing strong relationships with the right people.

Here are some areas to consider investing your energy in that will not only improve your overall performance as an educator, but also as a co-worker.

Develop a Unique Skill Set

It is always great to work in a building with educators who are specialists in different areas. Whether you have someone that is amazing with technology, strong in a particular curriculum area, great at organizing events, or even just really good at fixing the photocopier, these individuals' skill sets draw people to them.

Look for opportunities that will allow you to fulfill a need that the school has within your wheelhouse and something that you enjoy doing. Work on continually refining and improving this area so that you become seen as the expert or go-to person in your school.

Be willing to share these skills with others on staff. Whether it be presenting at staff meetings or offering individual support to those in need, take on that responsibility and make it something you are known for. People love to be in the company of other people who are skilled and willing to help.

Develop Strong Active Listening Skills

As someone who presents a lot to educators, active listening is one of the characteristics that I admire the most. I always appreciate people in the audience that you can tell are invested in the conversation. Through their posture, facial expressions and focus, they find a way to let you know that what you are saying is of interest to them and that they appreciate your time.

This is a skill that is much more difficult than it should be. With so many distractions and thoughts floating through our minds, we often struggle to stay actively engaged in the conversations we are in. This can leave a negative impression on those people who are willing to share their ideas and passions with you.

One of the most powerful exercises regarding active listening was one in which I was asked to identify if I was listening to respond or to understand in a variety of conversations. At first it was difficult to just listen, without the goal of responding. As I improved at listening to understand, the person I was partnered with noticed positive changes in my active listening skills.

Make it your goal to immerse yourself in conversations with educators you respect and want to develop stronger friendships with. Focus on becoming a more active listener in these conversations and watch new relationships form.

Become a Social Catalyst Risk Taker

Backpacking by myself around Australia taught me about the importance of putting myself out there and taking risks socially. Moving from hostel to hostel can be lonely if you are not willing to search out others to share your time with. That is why many hostels have bulletin boards that you can post on to connect with others staying there.

Two of the most memorable days on this trip were meeting Steve Irwin, The Crocodile Hunter, and attending the finals of the

Australian Rugby League. These amazing memories started when I took a risk and posted a note on one of these boards. By the end of each day, I was surrounded by a group of awesome people that I had not known hours before. We shared an incredible experience together that I will always remember, and it happened because I put myself out there.

As educators, we need to put ourselves out there if we want to develop the right team. There are so many ways to do this; create a book club, organize a social event, invite someone to collaborate on a project, etc. Don't just wait for others to set up social opportunities to get to know each other. Be willing to take risks in hopes of bringing people together and discovering new friendships.

Work on Positivity

All educators know that the system is not perfect, and neither are the students or administration. Some choose to focus on this, while others choose to focus on the millions of other great things that being an educator has to offer. Who do you think is happier? Who do you want to be friends with?

To attract positive people to us, we need to work on being positive. We need to train our brains to naturally pick out what is good more than we notice what is bad. The good news is that our brain is like a muscle that can be trained. Through building simple routines into our everyday, we can become more positive. The following chapter on routines will give practical ideas on how to build these happiness routines into our daily teaching.

INVEST IN OTHERS

As we begin to work on ourselves, others will naturally be drawn to us, and relationships will develop as a result. However, this is not enough. If we truly want to create strong, meaningful, and fulfilling friendships, we also must invest time and energy into people who inspire us and make us better.

Here are some job-embedded ways to help establish and build strong relationships with other educators that could one day become your Teacher Friends Forever!

1. Recognition

When searching for the happiest professions, hairdressers always rank near the top of the list.[40] Many factors contribute to this, but the one that stood out to me the most had to do with immediate positive feedback. At

the end of each haircut, hairdressers generally hear how much their client loves the haircut or how good it makes them feel. Every 20 minutes or so, they are recognized for their skill and effort, resulting in a positive boost to their mood.

Education on the other hand works much differently. Recognition does not often come daily- it usually comes in spurts at holidays or the end of the year if we are lucky. The best type of recognition for an educator comes many years after they have invested in a student when they find out that they were instrumental to a student's success or love of learning.

I believe that as educators, we need to fill the gaps in recognition by more consistently and effectively recognizing each other's accomplishments. If we leave this responsibility to students, parents and administration, it will often be missed. If we accept this responsibility as our own, we will help other educators feel more valued, and we will open up the opportunity to establish great friendships within the profession.

Random Acts of Recognition

The first time I heard the idea of Random Acts of Kindness, I thought it was genius. I began to build it into my relationships with friends, staff, and even strangers. When I was able to complete an Act of Kindness, it was amazing, but what I began to realize is that my completion rate was not very good. I would get a great idea on something kind to do for someone; however life would get in the way, and I would not get around to doing it.

So, I decided to simplify it for myself, and this is where I eventually came up with the spinoff idea that I now call Random Acts of Recognition. The major difference is that I act on authentic thoughts in the moment, in the easiest, most accessible way possible. Here are a couple of examples of what it might look like in education.

As I sit on my couch winding down from a long day, a thought about an amazing educator I worked with earlier in the week passes through my mind. Immediately, I will pick up my phone and send a text or email to that person. I quickly articulate the positive thought that I had and share it with them.

If I am watching an educator present at a conference or in a staff meeting and they inspire me or push my thinking, I make a of point of approaching them after to relay the positive thoughts that were going through my mind while they were speaking. If I do not get the opportunity, I send them a quick text or email to express my gratitude.

Too often, we have these positive thoughts but do not put them into action. These are missed opportunities in so many ways. I cannot begin to tell you the impact this has had on my relationships both inside and outside of education. For the purpose of this book, I will focus on how this has impacted my relationships within the profession and a couple realizations that I have come to.

Not Enough Recognition

The reactions of many educators to these acts of recognition speak for themselves. There is often this moment of disbelief and confusion as to why it is happening. People are just not used to receiving recognition out of the blue. Their next reaction is always one of gratitude and happiness.

I remember delivering a Random Act of Recognition to a presenter at a conference who was very nervous, but at the same time very inspiring. As I explained my positive thoughts to her about her presentation, she began to cry. When I asked why she was crying, she said, "It is just no one has ever taken the time to recognize all the hard work I have put into this."

This is not acceptable. As educators, we invest so much energy into what we do every day. We need more moments where we feel appreciated and recognized for our many talents and the extra time we invest in our students, school, and the profession as a whole.

Recognition Creates Relationships

I credit Random Acts of Recognition for the expansion of my social circle. Many of my new friends stem directly from one text or email that I sent based on an authentic thought.

For instance, I was at a district meeting, and a teacher received an award from the director for this amazing project she was working on at her school. I took a quick picture of the screen with her name on it so that I could remember it. When I got home, I emailed her, explaining how inspired I was by her work. She responded by inviting me to participate in the project that she was being recognized for. Years later, we are always in contact, I consider her a great friend, and I am a much better person and educator because I know her.

Making the effort and being vulnerable enough to act on positive thoughts can lead to the development of relationships that you might never have had the opportunity to nurture. You never know what can develop from one positive.

2. Making Time

Time is a significant factor when it comes to solidifying friendships and moving them forward. The research suggests that it takes around 50 hours of socializing to move from acquaintance to casual friend. It takes around 90 hours to become 'real' friends and around 200 hours to become close friends.[41]

Fortunately for educators, there are many opportunities throughout each day to connect, socialize and collaborate with our peers. Value these opportunities as something worth investing in, and make a point of carving out time in your busy schedule to nurture relationships that will increase your overall level of happiness.

Here are some ideas on how you can embed socializing into your work life so that you are getting what you need accomplished while at the same time investing hours into what could one day be your TFF.

Align Your Goals Inside of the Classroom

Most educators are involved in some type of Annual Learning Plan, where they set goals and create an action plan for themselves. If we are able to align our goals and learning with other educators who we enjoy being around, this will create more opportunities for us to invest valuable hours together in a productive way.

Through sharing valuable learning experiences and collaborating together, we are doing a lot more than just logging hours towards a friendship. We are developing trust, learning about each other and exploring commonalities that we share.

Several of my closest friendships in education stem back to co-planning lessons together as part of a learning team. Throughout this time together, we developed a deep mutual respect for the skills, dedication, and passion that each of us brought to the table.

Align Your Goals Outside of the Classroom

The positive effects of extracurricular activities on students have been well-documented. The statistics show significant improvement in grades, attendance, and overall satisfaction while at school.[42] There is also research to support that teacher job satisfaction is also positively affected by taking on the responsibility of leading extracurriculars. [43]

This is largely in part due to the increase in social interactions and the sense of belonging that participants experience with others. These benefits are not exclusive to just the student-teacher relationships that are formed. Many educators I have met attribute working together with other educators on extracurriculars as a pivotal milestone in their friendship.

In a profession where we spend the majority of our time isolated from our coworkers, extracurricular activities are a great opportunity to collaborate on a shared passion or goal. By committing to a club, team, or an event together, it ensures that you will carve out time in your busy day to enjoy the company of others. Not only that, it exposes us to meeting a variety of new people in a variety of settings and situations.

3. ONGOING SUPPORT

Let's be honest, teaching is hard. There are always a million things to do, and not enough time to do them. Not only that, there are days that do not go as planned, lessons that flop, and moments where nothing is going right. On these types of days, weeks, or months, what we need most is someone to be there for us.

Whether it is a pep talk, a resource, or advice, we need to have someone in our corner that will take the time out of their busy schedule to give us the support we need. Consistently being that person for someone is how you develop a close friendship.

Fortunately in education, a lot of our experiences and knowledge are transferable to other educators. We must be willing to share what we have and what we know. Working together is what makes this profession manageable.

RESOURCES

As educators, we are always creating and curating resources to help us deliver engaging and meaningful lessons. If you find something that you feel has really helped you in the classroom, look for opportunities to share with others on staff who might benefit as well. Even if you come across a great resource that does not fit with what you are teaching, share it with others on staff who would benefit from having access to it.

With the advancements in educational technology, it is now easier than ever to share resources. By developing skills around working online and housing your files in an online environment, you can easily share files and folders with the click of a few buttons. So much better than lending out our binder and never getting it back!

The act of sharing resources shows other staff members that you are generous, caring, and a team player. Creating this culture at work will eventually reduce your workload and provide support for you when it is needed.

KNOWLEDGE/EXPERTISE

Throughout our careers, we pick up many tricks along the way that help us become successful in the classroom. Whether it be an effective teaching strategy or a way to be more efficient at completing our report cards, these tricks help us do our job at a more productive level. Be generous with this knowledge when there is a need.

The key is to be attentive to the needs of other staff members. If you see a staff member struggling with something that you have worked through in the past, ask them if they would be open to hearing what worked for you. Try to approach them in a manner that you do not come off as abrasive. Done effectively, this could be a great way to spend quality time together, while at the same time helping them resolve the problem they are dealing with.

Meeting the need of another staff member does not always have to revolve around helping them. Sometimes just to be there to listen. There are times when you just need someone patient who is willing to listen as you work through it. Be that person. When you need someone to be there for you, they will hopefully return the favor.

INVEST

When you find someone who you enjoy getting to know and working with, invest extra time and effort developing that relationship. As the friendship grows, continue to do all of the things you were doing that contributed to the relationship's success. If by chance they leave and move on to another school, work even harder to keep them in your social circle. Teacher Friends Forever are worth every ounce of energy you put into them. They are an amazing investment in happiness.

Random Act of Recogition

1. Think of an educator that has inspired you over the last year.

2. When you thought of this person, why did they pop into your head? What have they done to be the first person that came to mind?

3. Now, pick up your device and send them a quick email, text or shout out on social media explaining that you were asked to think of an inspiring educator and that they came to mind. Then explain to them why.

4. Now that this message is sent, think of the following:

   ☺ How happy did you feel while you were creating this message?

   ☺ Were you smiling while you were doing it?

   ☺ How do you think they will feel when they receive this message?

   ☺ Are you excited to hear their response?

   ☺ How long did it take you to send this message?

   ☺ What impact did this short amount of time invested have on your relationship?

   ☺ What impact did this short amount of time invested have on your happiness?

5. Congratulations! You have just completed a Random Act of Recognition. It is that easy!

6. Now try a couple more. Spend 10 minutes sending messages to those you respect and admire!

TEAM:
POSITIVE PERSONAL LEARNING NETWORKS

"The most valuable resource that all teachers
have is each other. Without collaboration
our growth is limited to our own perspectives."
— *Robert John Meehan*

I want to start off this chapter by saying that nothing can replace the positive impact that face-to-face interactions have on our happiness. Technology may have made it easier to 'socialize,' however, it does not give us the same benefits as spending time with people that we enjoy and care about.[44]

That being said, social media platforms have become a way of life for many people. Studies have shown that the average person invests nearly two hours a day on social media.[45] The research also suggests that this time invested online is having negative effects on mental health, leading to anxiety, depression, and loneliness for many. [46]

However, this does not have to be the case. If used effectively, social media platforms can be a very powerful tool to inspire, connect and educate. If we are going to invest in screen time each day, we need to do so in a manner that contributes to our overall health and wellness. As educators, one of the most valuable ways to use technology is to create what is known as a Personal Learning Network (PLN).

WHAT IS A PLN?

The term Personal Learning Network or often referred to as Professional Learning Network, surfaced around the time that the internet was gaining popularity. With this increased ability to network, people began to realize the potential of connecting and sharing resources to support learning. Decades later, PLNs have become a haven for millions of educators.

Personal Learning Networks differ greatly from the type of Professional Development that is common in education. The learning is entirely in the hands of the learner. We get to choose which platform to use, what topics to explore, and what ideas that we would like to share. Not only that, we get to expand our network beyond the borders of the institution that employs us and have the opportunity to connect with educators all over the world.

Investing in a Personal Learning Network fulfills the need of autonomy for many educators. Often in education, our professional development is determined by the system in hopes of achieving specific goals. Developing a PLN is freeing for many educators. We have the ability to learn without limitations or expectations. We can change directions, follow our passion, and find our niche amongst other educators who we respect and who inspire us.

POSITIVE PLNS AND HAPPINESS

With happiness in mind, social media can be a very powerful tool. Like anything, it is how we use it that will determine its value. It is important to be very conscious of what type of media that we are exposing ourselves to and how this will affect our overall well-being. If we are constantly exposing ourselves to negative media, this will obviously have a negative impact on our perceptions and beliefs. However, if we carefully filter the media that we are digesting each day, we can use technology in a way that is positive and inspiring.

This all starts with creating a Positive Personal Learning Network around yourself. The people that you choose to let into your circle will determine the quality of the information that you receive. Make it your goal to connect with others who are happy, optimistic, and who post information that is uplifting. Invest time and energy into the people that love being educators, not ones that are constantly complaining and pointing out the negatives. This is much easier online than it is in a school setting — just unfollow!

Once you have established a Positive PLN, you now have a space where you can go to re-energize and be inspired. Not only that, this online community that you are building around yourself will be there for extra support, guidance, and professional development.

Over time, some of the connections that you have made with others may develop to the point where online friendships are established. You look forward to seeing them online and begin to connect directly with them to share ideas.

Although these relationships are not face-to-face, they will contribute to your overall experience as an educator. It gives you a sense of belonging and makes you feel connected to something bigger. You now have a place to meet many like-minded people who share your passion, value your ideas, and who are looking for the same things that you are... to be happy and impactful in education.

A Great Fit for Educators

As educators, there are countless ways that we can invest our time to become better at what we do. Taking into account the demands of this profession, PLNs become a viable option for those who are looking to engage in their own professional development. Here are some reasons that many educators have decided to use social media to help support their own learning.

Flexibility

The great part about going online to learn is that we can access it wherever and whenever it suits us. We have 24/7 access to a constant flow of information and ideas that can positively impact our ability to do our job. We can pick away at it throughout the day or invest a block of time. We get to choose whatever works best with our personality and schedule.

Quick Access to Global Support

Since there are so many educators using social media to connect with each other, it is quick and easy to move ideas throughout the profession. For instance, a study on Game-Based Learning analyzed a Twitter conversation over a 12-hour period. In this short amount of time, 110,000 people participated from 18 countries.[47] This speaks to the power, breadth, and potential that connecting online has in education.

There is a culture established in most online Personal Learning Networks that is based on helping and supporting others. People you have never met are willing to share resources, ideas, and experiences in hopes of making connections and expanding their impact. Due to the rapid movement of information, it is quick and easy to get the support you are searching for.

Cutting Edge Knowledge

As educators, we are constantly innovating and searching for new ideas. It is in our nature to want to 'creep' what others are doing in their classrooms to help us come up with our next big idea. Social media gives us an amazing glimpse into the best and next practices in all different aspects of education.

The design of most platforms promotes a constant flow of ideas that are current and trending. These websites are quick to maneuver and easy to search. If you want access to the newest information first, you can even follow and set notifications that will connect you instantly when it arrives.

Variety of Media

The idea of different learning preferences is widely accepted in education. However, this should not just be relevant for student learning. As educators, we must find the learning style that works best for us. Seeking professional learning online allows us to tap into a variety of different media efficiently.

For instance, I struggle to concentrate while reading plain text. My preference is to either watch a video or listen to podcasts or audio books. I enjoy when my PLN posts a video that inspires me, shares a great infographic or connects me to an interesting podcast that I can listen to while I drive. Regardless of your preference, you can easily find links to great content that will work best for you.

Creating Your PLN

When developing your Positive Personal Learning Network, try to keep in mind the following keys to help you get the most out of it:

1. Have fun and enjoy the process.
2. Take risks. Don't be afraid to put yourself out there.
3. Limit negative media and search out positive media.
4. Don't forget to invest in people, not just ideas.

Building Your Network

If you are new to the idea of developing a PLN online, here are some tips on how to get started:

Select a Platform:

There are many platforms that educators use to connect online. When trying to decide which one to use, ask friends and other educators that you respect what they are using. Then create an account and view their profile to see if you like the format and information that you see.

Bonus Tip: Twitter is one of the most popular microblogging platforms for educators. It is easy to use and a great starting point if you are unsure of where to start.

First Impression:

Invest time in setting up a great profile. Due to the quick moving nature of social media, make your profile interesting and ensure it connects well with others at a glance. Aim for a profile that is memorable, captures your passion as an educator, and includes your areas of interest.

Bonus Tip: Use the same profile picture if you are using multiple platforms to connect. This will make it easier for others to identify and connect with you.

Unique Username:

Often platforms will ask you to create a username or handle. Try to find something that is short, original, and easy to remember. As your network grows, you want to make it easy for others to connect and share information with you.

Bonus Tip: If all of the usernames that you are interested in are taken, try adding something short before or after it. For instance, you could try adding EDU to the end (i.e. @robdunlopEDU). It quickly lets others know that you are an educator.

Friend of a Friend:

Pay close attention to whom the people that you are following follow. By quickly scanning through their feed or going into their contacts, you will probably find others whom you share interests with. This is a great way to get you into a suitable PLN that is already started.

BONUS TIP: Once you add someone to your network, let them know that you are enjoying their posts by clicking like, sharing, or commenting on a post that made you interested in adding them to your contacts.

SHARE YOUR LEARNING:

Authors and educational leaders love when you share information that you learned from them. Posting your favorite quote from their book or sharing an insight that was inspired by them will often lead to them sharing your post. This is a quick way to get others with similar interests to connect with you.

BONUS TIP: Make sure you use their proper handle and/or hashtag when posting. This is what will alert them and their following that you have posted something that is promoting their ideas.

STAY ACTIVE:

To develop a strong PLN, you need to be active online. The more times that you click like or share a post will increase your likelihood of connecting with others. However, eventually move beyond this to creating your own posts and sharing your own ideas. It is also a great idea to ask questions, ask for help, and to give back by helping others.

BONUS TIP: When you are posting your ideas that you want to get out there, be cognizant of the time you are posting them. Because social media is often a scrolling news feed, posts can easily get buried if posted at the wrong time. One study showed that the best time for educators to post on Twitter was Saturday between 1 p.m. and 10 p.m. (CST).[48] Just pay attention to when your PLN is most active and try to post then if possible.

TAKE A HINT:

Social media platforms will usually suggest users that you might be interested in connecting with. Take time to find out why they are appearing on your list. It is often because you share contacts in common, or you have shown interest in similar content. These platforms are doing some of the work for you, take advantage of this generosity!

BONUS TIP: Keep a lookout for #FollowFridays. This is a great way to see who other educators enjoy following. If you want to take a risk, create your own #FollowFriday of your favorite members of your PLN!

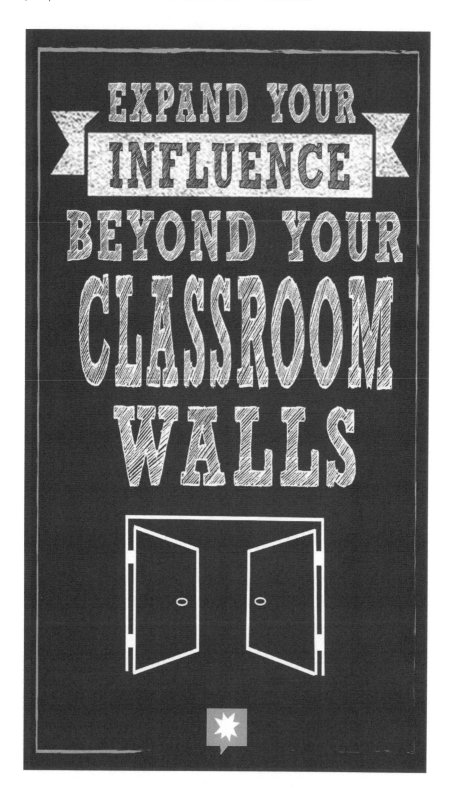

Looking for More?

Once you have grasped the basics of using social media to create your PLN, there are many other ways that you can delve deeper. Here are just a few of the ways to elevate your time online to a new level.

Join an Online Chat

Every night of the week, educators converge online to take part in chats on many different topics. Through the use of hashtags, members of the chat respond to questions that are being asked by the person moderating the chat. This is a fast paced way to communicate with very passionate educators who love to share their ideas and insights.

As you establish your PLN, you will begin to see these chats promoted online. Or, if you want to see what is available each night, just search 'Education Chats Schedule' in your browser.[49] This will give you a listing of all the chats that are running that night and the hashtag to find them. It is truly amazing to see how many chats are scheduled every night and the amazing variety of topics that there are to choose from.

I remember taking part in my first chat. I was literally sweating as I found it so exciting and engaging. I made the mistake of thinking that I needed to answer each question. My suggestion is only post when you have something that you really want to share. This frees you up to read the ideas of others in the chat. Taking the time to like, share and comment on what others are posting is a great way to connect with new educators.

If you are hesitant to join an educational chat, don't be. You can follow a chat without posting, and no one will know. Once you get more comfortable and are ready to join your first chat, be sure to introduce yourself, and admit that this is your first chat. Members of chats love when people post for the first time. You will be welcomed with open arms and instantly add to your PLN.

If you really enjoy the experience of being a part of a chat and want even more, create your own chat. It is easy to do. Just set a date, time, create a hashtag, and promote it within your PLN. This is a great first step to becoming an educational leader online.

Blogging

If you find that 280 characters are not enough for you to express your thoughts and ideas, consider starting a blog. This will give you the freedom to write as much as you need. As well, you will be able to keep all of your ideas organized and together.

Many educators start using a blog as a reflection tool or a place to express the ideas running wild in their heads. Some feel that it's therapeutic to write down their thoughts, while others are looking to expand their impact. Regardless of your motive, blogs offer a great place for educators to share their ideas with other educators.

Even if you are not ready to start blogging, you might find it beneficial to follow those who do. Connecting to bloggers through social media is a great way to keep up on what they are posting. It also introduces you to their PLN and many educators that share similar interests.

Remember that if you do start a blog, connect it to whatever social media platforms that you are using. That will give those who follow you access to your blog and a deeper insight into your ideas and passions.

TWEETUPS

A tweetup is an amalgamation of the words "tweet" and "meetup." This is what Twitter users do to transform their online connections into face to face meetings. Other platforms may have different names for it, but I think this one is the best.

My first experience with a Tweetup was very awkward- the reason being was that I never knew I was in one. I was at a conference, eating lunch. The table I sat at seemed to be all TFFs laughing and exchanging stories. They were really excited to be together, and I felt like an outlier not knowing anyone. As I listened in on their conversation, I realized that this was their first time meeting. They were all following each other on Twitter, but had never had the opportunity to meet. They decided to attend this conference where they could get together for the first time.

Eventually, I worked myself into the conversation. Within minutes, they all had their phones out, adding me to their social media. Quickly, I followed them back, and by the end of lunch, I was a part of their PLN. Since then, we have continued to stay in contact via Twitter and look forward to finding another opportunity to meet again.

If you have managed to build a great PLN around you, consider the idea of hosting a face-to-face meetup. Doing this will give you the benefits that only face-to-face contact can give you. Just find a time and place that is suitable for most, put it out there and see who shows up. It could bring you one step closer to finding another TFF!

Maximizing the Benefits of Your PLN

Investing time in developing a Personal Learning Network needs to be something that you do because you enjoy it. Your time spent online should be something that you look forward to and that you feel helps you as an educator. The people that you connect with daily should be ones that inspire you and push your thinking. Be patient and understand that it takes time to develop an amazing PLN, and if you stick with it, you will get there.

However, as your network grows ask yourself some key questions to help you get the most out of this experience. Here are some of those questions to keep in mind:

Are you investing too much time on PLN?

Always monitor how much time you are spending online. It is very easy to get so wrapped up in your PLN that you begin to drop the ball in other areas. Using social media sometimes results in becoming very distracted and can even distance yourself from your 'face-to-face' friends and family. Always make the people closest to you in your life a priority, and only invest time in your PLN that does not take away from those relationships.

How do I shape my PLN to best suit my needs?

There is a lot of trial and error in developing your PLN. Often you might follow another user based on one post you liked. However, from that point on, they are filling your feed with information that is not relevant to you. If that is the case, simply unfollow them. Don't worry, people will not be offended, it happens all of the time. You want to keep your news feed as interesting and positive as possible. By cleaning out your contact lists, it makes going online more efficient and meaningful. You can spend less time and get more out of it.

Are you giving back as much as you are taking?

At the beginning, it is natural to be tentative and passive when new to a platform. Give yourself that time to get a feel for what is going on in this new environment. Be mindful of the posts that you like, and feel are effective. When you are ready, take the leap and begin to share. Just like the people you enjoy following, you have many great ideas and insights that are worthy.

It is much like any relationship. For it to work effectively, both parties need to be willing to put themselves out there, contribute ideas and reciprocate the energy that is invested. The more of you that you invest in your PLN, the quicker it will grow and the more positive impact it will have on you.

Does your PLN and time online make you happier?

Our time online should be a positive experience. We should feel inspired when using social media to connect. If we are not, we need to change the way we are using it. For instance, this might not be for you if you feel that you are constantly comparing yourself to others, and it is making you feel worse. Always remember that what you are seeing is a small window into each educator. They are usually showcasing their best ideas or strengths. Enjoy these posts for what they are, and do not get down on yourself. That is not what having a PLN is all about.

See You Online

Whether you've had a PLN for a while or are just about to create one because of this chapter, I hope that you find a PLN that you truly enjoy, and that makes you happier. See you online!

Keep track of how much time you spend on social media over the course of one week. Be honest!

MONDAY	TUESDAY	WEDNESDAY	THURSDAY	FRIDAY	SATURDAY	SUNDAY

Record your total number of minutes you spent on social media throughout the week in the box below.

_____ MINUTES

REFLECTION QUESTIONS:

Is the time that you are currently investing in social media making you happier?

When you look at the amount of time that you have spent on social media, do you feel that it is a good investment?

Can you identify content from the last week that has inspired you or helped you?

What have you posted that could inspire or help others?

Have you built a community around yourself online that helps you grow and be happier?

ROUTINES:
Nudges, Triggers & Cues

"You'll never change your life until you change something you do daily. The secret of your success is found in your daily routine."
- John C. Maxwell

What is the first thing you do after you get out of bed in the morning? Which shoe do you put on first? What is the first thing you do when you get to your desk? You probably had to stop and think about each of these questions, but why? You do them almost every day.

It is because these are habits that have formed over many years, and they occur automatically without much thought. Research has shown that around 40% of our actions each day are habits.[50] They are so ingrained in what we do that performing them requires little brain activity or decision making.

Think of driving to work each day. Have you ever got lost in thought to the point you forgot part of the drive? If so, think about all of the habits that needed to occur for that to happen. You turned on the right streets, stopped in the right places, and followed numerous rules of the road with very little thought.

Now reflect on how much focus was needed when you were first learning to drive. It seemed overwhelming switching between the gas and brake pedal, staying in the middle of the road, indicating at each turn, monitoring your speed, reading the traffic signs and checking all three mirrors. However, through organizing your actions into routines and repeating them many times, you eventually got to the point where you could drive on autopilot.

Happiness Routines

Before something becomes a habit, it is part of a routine. This is a sequence of actions that is regularly followed. As educators, we know the importance of establishing routines. We invest a great deal of effort at the beginning of each year setting up classroom routines in hopes that they will eventually become habits for our students. We do this because we know that it will increase the likelihood of them succeeding in our class.

The same goes for happiness in education. We can build more joy in our daily routines to ensure that our days are filled with experiences that we enjoy and that contribute to our overall well-being.

The first step to infusing more happiness into your workday is to take the time to reflect on your daily routines. When doing so, consider each activity and the emotions that accompany it. Try to identify times of the day that you feel you are just going through the motions and getting little enjoyment from. Look to make changes there first.

For instance, let's go back to the drive to work. It is well documented that the longer a commute to work, the less likely you are to be happy.[51] Overall, people do not get much satisfaction from the drive to and from work. If this is you, then try to make changes to this routine that will bring you more enjoyment.

I used to drive to work mindlessly every day through the heart of the city. By the time I arrived at work, I was frustrated by slow drivers and red lights. However, I continued to take the same route each day because it was the most direct route.

One day I was alerted that there was an accident, so I needed to take an alternate route. The road I decided to take winded along a beautiful canal surrounded by trees and nice scenery. Although this route took me an extra 5 minutes, I arrived at work relaxed and happy. By making this simple change to my routine, I was able to start my workday off with a more positive attitude and mindset.

At one point, my role changed and required me to drive substantial distances between schools each day. I did not look forward to the drives and often found myself navigating through songs on the radio that annoyed me. The more I drove, the more this frustrated me. The drives were the most unproductive and least enjoyable part of each day. Then I discovered audiobooks.

From that point on, I was excited about the idea of driving. I began to look forward to the longer drives so that I could immerse myself in the content of the book I was listening to. Often, I would sit in the parking lot for a couple of extra minutes waiting until the author completed a thought or chapter. Over the course of that year, I read (well listened to) over 25 books that inspired me.

Making changes to our routines and habits can have a profound effect on our overall happiness. It is important that we analyze our daily routines and look for opportunities to infuse parts of our day with things that bring us joy.

Learning from the Happiest and Healthiest

Through his work with National Geographic, Dan Buettner has given us insight into the lives of the happiest and healthiest people in the world.[52]

These regions are of great interest because their population lives longer with less disability. Their elderly population remains active into their 80s and 90s, many of whom are living to 100 years of age. Research suggests that our genes only account for 20% of our life expectancy; the rest is based on our daily routines, habits, and environment.[53]

Based on his extensive research of these regions, the author is now transforming communities throughout the United States using principles learned from how the people in these regions live their lives. For instance, in Minnesota, they were able to increase projected life expectancy by 2.9 years and decrease health claims by 49%.[54] In three cities in California, they dramatically dropped health risks associated with obesity and smoking, saving $12 million in healthcare.[55] All just by making changes to their daily routines.

What I found most interesting about this was the idea of making changes to the environment that would nudge people into making healthier decisions. Developing and sticking to new routines can be very challenging. However, if we are able to build cues or triggers into our day that initiate healthier habits, we are much more likely to succeed.

Understanding Habits

What if we were to apply the idea of nudges into helping us create happier routines into our day? Would it work? Yes. However, there are two more aspects that we must consider. First, we must understand how habits are formed. Second, we must know how to change pre-existing habits.

A habit is made up of three essential parts; the cue, the routine, and the reward. The cue is responsible for triggering what habits to use. These cues can be categorized into the following:[56]

1. Location
2. Time
3. Mood
4. Thoughts
5. Preceding Action
6. Social Interaction

The cue will initiate the routine, which is the behavior itself. Finally, there is a reward. This reward will help your brain determine if that routine is worth remembering for the future.

For instance, when I am bored, I tend to snack. The cue for this habit is boredom (mood). This triggers me to rummage through my cupboards looking for something, anything to eat. The reward is that I get a break from the task that I was losing interest in doing. If you carefully analyze your habits you will realize that they follow this cycle.

Charles Duhigg, the author of The Power of Habits, states, "that simply understanding how habits work - learning the structure of the habit loop- makes them easier to control."[57] By breaking a habit down into these three components, we can begin to make changes to pre- existing habits or learn to develop new habits.

MAKING NEW HABITS

The rest of this chapter will be filled with ideas on new routines you can add to your workday that will lead to more happiness. When implementing these new routines, ensure you trigger each routine with a cue, and complete the loop by having a clear reward.

The reward is a crucial part of the habit loop. Each time a reward is received, our brain is stimulated by a pleasure response.[58] If this routine is repeated regularly with that specific reward, you will eventually begin to develop a craving. It is this craving that will help you eventually turn your routine into a habit.[59]

One of the habits that has had the greatest impact on my overall happiness was Random Acts of Recognition. The cue for this action was an authentic thought about someone. This thought would trigger me to immediately send a text or email. Finally, the reward was the anticipation of them receiving the recognition or their reply.

Each positive response to this type of recognition strengthens the connection between the cue and the reward. Eventually, I began to look forward to opportunities to send communication of this nature. Now it is just part of what I do daily. It requires very little discipline or planning, but has an amazing impact on my life.

Changing Old Habits

If we are struggling to find contentment in our jobs, chances are that we have developed habits over the years that are not contributing to our happiness. It is important that we take the time to closely analyze these habits and create a plan to alter them.

The first step is to correctly identify the cues and rewards. Because these habits are so automatic, we generally do not invest energy thinking about them. This is part of the problem. We need to determine when and why they are occurring and what reward helped them become part of our daily routine.

Let's say that you have developed a habit of venting your frustrations at the end of each workday. The cue could be a thought about an event that frustrated you. These thoughts trigger you to find someone that will listen to you vent about this situation. The reward is that you feel a sense of relief by getting these negative emotions out.

By simply understanding this loop, it gives you the power to be able to change it. The Golden Rule of Habit Change says that the most effective way to shift a habit is to select and change only one part of the loop.[60] In this situation, it makes the most sense to keep the cue and reward and to change the routine.

For instance, when you have negative thoughts such as these, substitute a new routine that will give you the same sense of relief, but also improve your overall well-being. You might need to try several different routines to find the one that works best. Perhaps try to substitute in yoga, kickboxing, breathing techniques, journaling, etc. If one of these routines helps to diffuse your frustration and allows you to move past the negative parts of your day, then it will most likely stick as a new habit. This is largely in part because it has the same cue and reward.

Habit Pairing

When trying to adopt new routines and habits, try pairing a habit that you enjoy with one that you do not. For instance, I do not like doing dishes. That was until I paired it with watching inspiring videos online.

One day I stumbled on the 'Watch" video tab at the bottom of my Facebook app. Essentially, it cues up videos for you based on your clicks and likes. I had a huge load of dishes I needed to do before my wife returned home. So, I started watching inspiring auditions on shows like America's Got Talent and X-Factor while doing the dishes. Now I actually love doing dishes; every time I do them I watch these videos- leaving me feeling inspired and happy.

Look for easy ways to pair what you do not like to do or struggle to fit into your day, with activities that you enjoy. Whether you are stretching or exercising while watching TV or listening to podcasts while doing yard work, find the combination that works best for you.

KEYSTONE HABITS

If you were to look at changing habits as an investment in yourself, which habits would give you the greatest return? The answer is keystone habits. These are habits that lead to the development of other healthy habits. They can spark a cascade of positive changes that ripple through many aspects of your life. Many of the positive outcomes that come from these keystone habits often seem unrelated to the habit itself.

The most common example of a keystone habit is exercise. It is conclusive to say that exercise has a direct positive effect on one's overall well-being. However, what makes this a keystone habit is that it also affects other habits and routines that are not related.

For instance, people who exercise:[61]

- Eat healthier
- Are more productive
- Smoke less
- Are more patient
- Use credit less

Another example is making your bed. Research shows that making your bed every morning starts a chain reaction that helps other habits take hold. It is your first win of the day and will lead to many other habits that are not directly related, such as:[62]

- Increased productivity
- Improved well-being
- Better at sticking to a budget
- Liking your job
- Exercising regularly

Charles Duhigg explains that a keystone habit is much more than just a change in behavior- it is a change in how we see ourselves. Creating habits in key areas of our lives that build our confidence, redefine us as a person, and/or improve our overall self-efficacy, will have a trickle-down effect on many other of the habits that impact our lives.

He also goes on to say that, "anything can become a keystone habit if it has the power to make you see yourself in a different way."[63] As educators, we need to invest time and energy into developing habits that we are proud of, and that define us in a way that is positive and impactful for our students.

Find What Works for You

It would be great if there was a surefire way to establish and transform healthy routines into habits, but there is not. How we develop habits and how we get them to stick is unique for everyone. Our personality plays a major role in how we decide to approach habit change.

For instance, some people will experience the most amount of success starting with small changes and gradually building on their successes. Whereas others will be more comfortable overhauling their old habits and replacing them with new ones. Either way, it is important to understand your relationship with your habits.

Take time to analyze your current routines and habits. Then, monitor carefully the habits that you feel are holding you back from being happier and healthier. By monitoring your habits, you are more likely to begin to understand them and therefore be more equipped to change them.

As you implement changes into your routines and habits, look at everything as a learning experience about yourself. Play around with what works and what does not work. Try to figure out what cues are effective and what rewards are most likely to motivate you to continue these habits. Find people who support these changes in your lifestyle and who celebrate with you as you succeed.

Look at this as a journey. Do not buy into the idea that a habit takes 21 days to form because researchers have dispelled this myth.[64] Do not put an expiry date on your efforts — continue to work, adapt and pursue habits that in the long run will change your life for the better.

But Wait... Don't Get Too Comfortable

With all of this focus on creating and changing habits, one might think that this habituation is the goal. However, it is not that simple. The more automatic a habit becomes, the weaker the emotional response.[65] If our goal is to experience more happiness, then we need to monitor when this habit begins to lose its effectiveness.

For instance, at one point I decided to write down what I was grateful for each day. At the beginning, this was a very powerful way to help me develop a greater appreciation for my life. Eventually, it developed into

a habit. I started to realize that I was beginning to just go through the motions, writing similar things every day. I was not getting the positive spike in mood that I was for the first several months. I could not understand why.

That is until I read the book *Making Habits, Breaking Habits* by Jeremy Dean. In the last chapter, he explains the relationship between habits and happiness. He stresses the importance of creating 'little variations in regular routines.'[66] By doing so, you are able to capture the benefit of it being a habit, while at the same time still benefitting emotionally.

Since I already had the habit of practicing gratitude in place, I decided to make a variation to this routine. I decided to try the idea of a gratitude walk. So instead of journaling what I was grateful for, I would go on a short walk and think about it. Just this small variation on how I went about practicing gratitude brought back my emotional connection to this habit.

That is why we must constantly monitor what we are doing is still moving us towards becoming happier. In the following chapter, there will be many ideas of possible ways to find more joy in education. Hopefully some of these ideas give you a starting point or area of focus. But don't just take these ideas as they are, use them to formulate your own ideas and make variations to them so that they work for you!

Routines and Habits

1. Make a detailed chronological list of your average day. Try to focus on routines. Things that you do everyday, such as brushing your teeth, your drive to work, what you do first when you get into school, what you do at lunch, on breaks, after school, etc...

2. Put a " ✔ " besides the routines that you enjoy the most.

3. Put an " ✘ " beside the routines that take away from your enjoyment of the day.

4. Select one routine on this list that you would like to alter or eliminate?

5. Complete the cycle below by filling in the trigger, routine and reward for this routine.

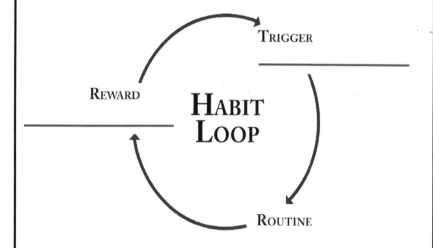

6. Now that you have the habit cycle for this routine, play with different ways of changing either the cue or reward to help alter this routine to bring you more happiness.

ROUTINES:
Teacher Happiness Routines

"Happiness is a habit- cultivate it."
— Elbert Hubbard

The life of an educator is very routined. We have loud bells that ring to tell us when to start the day, when to switch classes, when to eat our lunch, and when to dismiss our students. Then we build more routines into our lessons in the hope of making everything run smoothly and to help us accomplish our lesson goals. This intense structure not only helps us stay on track, it also presents us with a great opportunity to systematically build more happiness into each day.

I often think that most educators enter this profession because they either like or need structure in their lives. By the time we graduate and enter this profession, we have spent approximately 15 years responding to bells and attending classes. Once we become educators, we can take control over these routines and use the structure of each day to our benefit.

This starts with developing a greater awareness of your routines and habits. As you begin to analyze your daily actions, be on the lookout for opportunities to make small changes in habits that will have a great impact on your well-being and mood.

These changes should be unique to you and your personality. What works for one person might not work for the next. However, there are six common areas that will help most educators find more happiness at work. They are: Self-care, Mindfulness and Gratitude, Positive Intake, Socialization, Signature Strengths/Skills and Kindness

As you read through this chapter, reflect on your typical day and look for opportunities to make changes that will bring you more happiness. Try some of the ideas presented in this chapter or use these ideas to spark ,changes in routines that will work for you. As you begin to make changes, reflect on the overall impact they are having on you. By becoming more aware of these positive changes, you are more likely to turn them into a positive habit.

1. SELF-CARE

"Self-care is giving the world the best of you, instead of what's left of you."
— Katie Reed

The more I work with educators, the more I realize self-care is something we struggle with the most. We dedicate our lives to helping others, but in the process, we forget to take care of ourselves. We become last on a long list of priorities, and this eventually takes a toll on our overall well-being.

Although we often do this for our students, it is not what is best for them. What students want and need is a teacher who is happy and loves coming to work each day. A teacher who takes care of themselves, so that they can better take care of their class. The common analogy is that of a caring adult who takes oxygen first in an emergency, in order to more effectively help others.

I believe that for the most part we, as educators, know and understand the importance of self-care. I think we have an understanding of where we need to improve, and I believe most of us theoretically know how to go about it. So that brings us to the question, why do we consistently neglect our self-care as educators?

PERMISSION

As part of an educator wellness retreat, we invited a social worker to do a presentation on self-care. Throughout his 25 years in social work, he had the opportunity to work with many educators who struggled to find joy and balance. Not only that, he was married to a teacher who gave him an even greater insight into the profession.

The audience was engaged as he went through a list of advice regarding self-care for educators. A lot of the list were things that most of us already knew. For instance, the importance of proper sleep habits, healthy eating, moderation, and things of that nature. The interesting part for me came after the presentation while we were on break.

I engaged in a conversation with a group of educators who were discussing the information he presented. I asked them if they felt that this was of benefit to them and if we should bring him back next year. Overwhelmingly, they agreed that it was important and that we should have it every year. When I asked why, two things came out. First, they said

that they needed a reminder of what they should be doing to take care of themselves. Secondly, they felt like they were given permission to include more self-care into their lives.

I thought it was very powerful that we feel the need for permission when it comes to self-care. For many of us, there is guilt attached to putting our well-being in front of others. Carving out time in our schedules to do something for ourselves gets lost in the chaos of the day and the needs of our students. Often this leads to us feeling worn down, frustrated, and deprived. All of which takes away from our ability to work to our potential.

It was not until I read *Braving the Wilderness* by Brené Brown, that I realized what we need most is not the permission of others, it is the ability to give ourselves permission.[67] She has an amazing strategy that she uses in her own life that fits perfectly into education, permission slips!

Permission Slips

As educators, we send home hundreds of permission slips throughout our career, but maybe it is time to write some for ourselves. By putting our thoughts on paper, it often helps us put them into action. If you are struggling with self-care and making yourself a priority, try giving yourself permission by writing it down.

For instance:
- I give myself permission to unplug from work every night.
- I give myself permission to go for more walks.
- I give myself permission to go to bed at a reasonable time.
- I give myself permission to pursue interests outside of education.
- I give myself permission to say no when I have too much on my plate.
- I give myself permission to make mistakes.
- I give myself permission to not feel guilty for taking care of myself.
- I give myself permission to be happy.

Once you give yourself permission to invest in you, it is time to look closely at three keystone habits that might be affecting you the most: sleep, physical activity, and nutrition.

SLEEP

How many hours of sleep do you get each night? The recommended amount of sleep for a healthy adult is a minimum of seven hours.[68] A study at Ball State University has shown that 43% of teachers get 6 hours or less.[69]

For some people, that might be enough, but for most of us this will leave us feeling tired and sluggish.

We are fortunate as educators that we generally work dayshift. This gives us an advantage when it comes to our sleep routines. By having a consistent start time to our day, we have the ability to make adjustments and decisions that will help us feel much more rested. Here is a list of suggestions that might help you get that much-needed sleep you deserve after a long day of teaching.

RISE AND SHINE
Even on the weekends! Try to wake up at the same time on the weekends. Not only does it make it easier to wake up on Mondays for work, it also helps improve digestion, immunity, productivity, concentration and emotional stability.[70]

CAFFEINE CUTOUT
Avoid caffeine after 2pm. Sleep research shows that caffeine has 'disruptive effects' on sleep patterns if taken six hours prior to bedtime.[71]

DO NOT DISTURB
On your device, you can schedule it to automatically go into Do Not Disturb mode each night. This will save you from ruminating on an email while you are trying to get to sleep.

SCREEN CURFEW
The blue light emitted by screens "restrains the production of melatonin." This makes it hard to fall and stay asleep. It is recommended to have 30 minutes without screen time before bed.[72]

DIM THE LIGHTS
Slowly dim the lights throughout the evening. Dimming the lights signals your body to begin slowing down and preparing for bedtime.[73]

WORK BACKWARDS FROM BEDTIME
Figure out when you need to go to bed to get your seven-plus hours that you need. Plan your night backward so that you always start your bedtime routine at the same time.

SET A BEDTIME ALARM
Set an alarm on your device to signal when you should start your routine (turn devices off, dim lights, brush teeth, etc.).

FINAL BREATHS

Take a couple deep breaths once you get into bed. This will help to relax you to sleep.

PHYSICAL ACTIVITY

Marking, planning, coaching, and family commitments can make it difficult to find time to make it to the gym or to jump on a treadmill. Let's face it, by the time the evening comes around, energy can be in short supply. That is why we educators should try fitting more physical activity into our workday.

The ironic part about exercise is that the more energy we expend, the more energy we have. By starting our day with physical activity or building it into our established routines, we get the boost we need and the exercise our body needs. Here are some ideas to try at your school.

ACTIVE DUTY

Supervision duty can often be something that you dread. However, it is the perfect opportunity to squeeze in activity throughout the day. By remaining active throughout each break, you are taking advantage of this time and building more activity into your day.

The Center for Disease Control suggests at least 150 minutes of moderate activity a week.[74] If you convert this to steps, it works out to around 10,000 per day. On an average supervision duty that lasts 15 minutes, it would be realistic to take around 1500 steps if we kept moving. Doing this each day, we would walk almost four extra miles each week. Not only would this increase our overall activity, it would also help us cover more ground on duty and give us that extra boost of energy that we need mid-day.

Using a step counter such as a Fitbit or Smartwatch is a great way to track our activity level each day. Not only that, it acts as a great motivator. Watching our overall number of steps increase by making small changes such as moving more on duty, will encourage us to look for other ways throughout the school day to achieve our activity goals.

FREE GYM MEMBERSHIP

As educators, we all have free gym memberships and do not realize it. The school gymnasium can be an amazing space for educators to increase their overall activity levels throughout each day.

Whether you are sneaking in early to go for a walk before school or booking time throughout the day to be active with staff and/or students, it is a valuable resource that is often underused by most staff.

Having access to an indoor space such as a gymnasium in your workplace increases the likelihood of developing physical activity routines. A common barrier to making it to the gym is location. The thought of driving across town and fighting traffic after work can often deter us from wanting to go. The easier we make it, the more likely it will be to occur. That is why working out at school might be the answer.

Eliminate even more obstacles by keeping everything you need to exercise at school. Keep your gym bag somewhere that you can see it at work. This will act as the trigger you need to turn this routine into a habit.

Movement Breaks

For many students, sitting in a desk too long can make it difficult to concentrate and often affects their productivity. Building in short movement breaks throughout the day is a great way to keep them motivated and is another opportunity to build more activity into our day. By participating along with students, we are getting the same benefits as they are.

In Ontario, the Ministry of Education created the Daily Physical Activity Policy to ensure that "elementary students have a minimum of 20 minutes of moderate to vigorous physical activity each school day."[75] As educators, this is an opportunity for us to engage in more activity as well. Work on building this time into your timetable in a way that works for both you and your students. Find activities that you can lead and participate in that everyone can enjoy and benefit from.

As well, look for opportunities to embed activities in your lessons. For instance, take nature walks in science or do physical coding activities in math that get everyone moving. These small changes throughout the day can have a major impact on your overall well-being.

Extracurricular Activity

Making commitments to increase the physical activity of others is a great way to make being more active a priority in our schedule.

By volunteering our time to coach a team, run yoga sessions or start a walking club, we are creating the opportunity to become more active. The next step is to increase our involvement in the activity. By participating with the students and/or staff, we are setting a great example while at the same time getting in our physical activity.

The key is to find an activity that you enjoy and share that passion with others. For instance, I was in a school where a teacher organized a staff/student volleyball game twice a week. The attendance was always amazing. During lunch breaks, the participants built relationships with both staff and students while being more active.

NUTRITION

I am fortunate to be married to a dietitian. We often talk about the importance of food in relation to our mood. How and when we eat throughout the day can have a major impact on how we feel. As educators, we are lucky that the structure of our day fits nicely with good eating habits. Having the opportunity to eat at the same time each day helps with digestion, energy levels, and planning of meals.

To fuel our bodies for success, we must respect the impact that food has on our overall well-being. Here are some ideas for healthier eating habits my wife and I came up with that would help educators develop healthier eating routines at work.

BREAKFAST PROGRAM FOR EDUCATORS

Breakfast programs are becoming a thing in many schools across the world, and for good reason. Many educators see first hand the impact that not eating breakfast has on their students. By starting their day with a healthy meal, students are more productive, learn better, and feel better throughout the day.[76]

Although we see this as being vital for our students, many adults do not transfer this importance to themselves. Research shows that 10% of Americans skip breakfast every day[77] and 40% of Canadians report skipping breakfast throughout the week.[78] Teaching requires too much energy to start each day without eating. Invest time each morning eating a healthy breakfast to ensure that you are showing up to school energized and ready to work to your potential for your students.

If you struggle to fit breakfast into your morning routine, try some of the following tips:

- Keep breakfast in mind when you grocery shop.
- Try to eat within 1.5 hours of being awake.
- Prep breakfast the night before (i.e., cut up fruit, prep ingredients).
- Set out bowls and utensils the night before to trigger habit.
- Wake up 5-10 minutes early, so you are not rushing out the door.

You Can Write a Day plan, You Can Write a Meal Plan

Just as our lessons are better when they are thought out, so is our eating. As educators, we get good at planning out each week. Knowing what we are doing and having the materials we need gives us a sense of relief, and in the end is much easier. We need to apply this understanding to our meal planning.

Often when we wait until the last minute to decide what to eat, we don't make the best decisions. Meal planning makes eating healthier, easier and can save you time and money. Not only that, it can reduce stress around constantly scrambling to figure out the next meal. Here are some tips to help you build meal planning into your habits:

- Create a shopping list and stick to it.
- Write down on a weekly calendar so that you can look back for ideas.
- Create a list of quick and easy, healthy go-to meals.
- Plan for leftovers. Making extra portions for the next day's lunch saves you time and stress in the morning.
- Build in healthy snacks throughout the day that are easy to eat on the run if busy.

Pack It and Eat It

If you have invested time packing a healthy lunch, you might as well eat it. It requires a lot less discipline and effort eating lunch at work than it does at home. It is prepared, easy to access, and there are likely no other options — unless that is, you steal from the lunches of others.

Commit to one simple rule — eat the lunch that you pack. If you can commit to this rule, it will help you to fight off other temptations that are less healthy and allow you to set yourself up for success. To help make eating the lunch that you packed easier to do, here are some tips:

- Invest in a nice lunch box/bag system to keep food cold and easier to bring with you.
- Purchase nice containers that are easy to clean and pack.
- Keep nice utensils, plates, etc. at work to make it convenient to eat.
- Keep condiments, pepper, and other garnishes at work to ensure you can add more flavor if needed.
- Pack enough food, so you feel satisfied.
- Pack lunches that you look forward to eating.

Rotating Lunches

In some of the happiest places in the world, families work together to cut down the amount of effort needed to make meals and to bring everyone together. Each night a family prepares a meal for several other families. The following night another family prepares a meal for the group. Each family has an opportunity to cook and enjoy the cooking of others.

I cannot count how many educators I have talked to that do not like making lunches. The monotony of making meals gets tiring and frustrating. It is difficult to come up with new ideas that are fun, exciting, and that you look forward to eating. Educators who feel this way should bond together and set up rotating lunches. Ideally, if you had five friends on staff who buy in, you would only be responsible for one lunch a week!

When it is your turn to make lunch, it is more fun and rewarding. You will be more motivated knowing that your co-workers are going to enjoy what you bring. Not only that, it is easy to make a greater number of portions than it is to come up with many different lunches. If the group gets really into it, this could transform into a time that you look forward to each day.

The most important connection to happiness is that it will bring you together each day to socialize and share each other's company. You will have a lot to talk about, and this will give you a chance to have a true break from the day.

If every day is too much, find friends who are interested and select certain days of the week that work for the group. This way, you get a small break from planning lunches and can still have control over some of the lunches you bring.

By helping others to establish healthier habits that are making them happier, you are also increasing your likelihood of success. Working together on common goals can be very motivating, and it can give you the support that you need to be successful.

As you begin to make self-care a priority in your life, invite others to join you in your journey. Not only will this make it more fun, you will also develop deeper relationships with others on staff. There is a lot of enjoyment to be found in developing friendships around healthy habits.

Self-care Permission Slip

I, _____ , give myself permission
to take care of myself by _____

_____

_____

Signature, _____

Self-care Permission Slip

I, _____ , give myself permission
to take care of myself by _____

_____

_____

Signature, _____

Self-care Permission Slip

I, _____ , give myself permission
to take care of myself by _____

_____

_____

Signature, _____

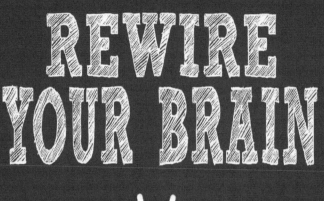

2. MINDFULNESS/GRATITUDE

"The more grateful I am, the more beauty I see."
— Mary Davis

As educators, it is easy to create a habit of never stopping. With so many students, so many needs and so many expectations, it can be hard to take a break. Before we know it, the day is done, and we find our coffee half-finished beside our to-do list that remained untouched. For many of us, this is the reality of teaching, but it does not have to be.

We need to give ourselves permission to slow down. Often we are scared to stop in case the pile gets higher, and we get further behind. We are racing to keep up with an endless amount of work that needs to be done. In doing so, we are missing out on many great moments and burning ourselves out.

THE PRODUCTIVITY TRAP

Ironically, not stopping is not the most productive way to go about this workload. There is ample research to support that being more mindful is the antidote. Simply put, mindfulness is the ability to be aware of our thinking. This increased awareness of ourselves and our environment has been proven to:[79]

- Increase productivity
- Improve decision-making
- Improve the immune system
- Increase clarity in thinking and perception
- Improve mood
- Improve memory
- Improve attention span

The benefits of mindfulness can have a significant overall impact on preventing workplace burnout and increasing overall performance. For instance, a study of over 12,500 employees at Aetna, a life insurance company, found decreased stress levels by 28% and improved productivity by 62 minutes/week, simply from taking short breaks to center themselves throughout the day.[80]

For many educators, this will seem counterintuitive. We have convinced ourselves that we need to be busy all of the time and that slowing down is a weakness. I know that I used to take great pride in labeling myself as "someone who was good at multitasking." It made me feel that I was getting more accomplished in a shorter amount of time. However, research states the opposite. Studies have shown that multitasking (or Task-Switching, as researchers put it), can decrease your productivity by up to 40%.[81]

By practicing being more mindful, we are training our brains to be more aware. This, in turn, helps us to focus our attention, eliminate distractions, and complete tasks with more efficiency and accuracy.

MINDFULNESS AND HAPPINESS

When neuroscientists want to study happiness in the brain, they look at the prefrontal cortex. This is the area of your brain that lights up with activity when experiencing positive emotions. Studies show that practicing mindfulness dramatically increases the activity in this part of the brain. The research also shows that the more we practice being mindful, the greater the benefit to our mood and mental health.[82]

The goal is to focus on being in the moment. Overall, people are happiest here. A Harvard study of over 15,000 people concluded that we are happiest when our minds are not wandering, especially if we are thinking pleasant thoughts. In this state, we experience less stress and more enjoyment.[83]

YOUR MINDFUL JOURNEY

Becoming more mindful is something that we need to train our brains to do. We need to build it into our daily routines to ensure that we are making time for it. Practicing mindfulness can range anywhere from taking deep breaths to full on meditation. It is something that can be very simple and quick or something that you can invest deeply into. The key is consistency.

As educators, we can look for opportunities to build mindfulness into our daily practice. Whether at home or at school, find time each day to develop a greater awareness of your thoughts, senses, and environment. Here are some ideas on how you can start.

START YOUR DAY OFF RIGHT

JUST ONE MORE MINUTE

Prior to getting out of bed in the morning, take an extra minute to lie in bed. Focus on your breathing; feel your body rise and fall with each breath. Try to avoid thinking about the rest of the day, just focus on your breathing. If you have young kids, this probably won't work for you. So you will need to try again later!

Shower Escape

Try the shower. It can be a great place of solitude and refuge in a busy home. Use this time to be present and focus on the different sensations affecting your body — the warmth of the water, the texture of the soap, the feeling of water hitting your skin, the aromas in the air, etc. Not only is this relaxing, but it is also training your brain to be more in the moment and in tune with your body.

Mindful Breakfast

Start your day off right by setting aside time to eat a mindful breakfast. Often, we rush through breakfast and rarely enjoy it. We get in the habit of checking our phones or watching TV while we eat. Try to make this time about being mindful of the food you are eating. Focus on the smell, the taste, and the textures of the food you are consuming. Try to notice flavors or sensations that you have missed in the past. This makes breakfast more enjoyable and helps improve your mindfulness.

Great Parking Spot

If it was a crazy morning and you could not find peace and quiet, try the parking lot. Before you throw it in park and jump out of the car, take a moment to take a deep breath and enjoy the silence. Or if that does not work for you, put on a song that you love and close your eyes. Focus on only the song. Try to feel the beat, the sound of each instrument or listen carefully to each word. This is your final opportunity to center yourself before the day starts.

Teach, Practice and Learn Together

Start Breathing

Start each day having students focus on their breathing. Breath is the starting and finishing point for all types of meditation. In a comfortable position, have students breathe slowly in and out. Have them focus on each breath by placing their hand on their chest or stomach. Encourage them to try to only focus on their breathing and nothing else. If you want to try something different, google five

finger breathing. It is another great activity to do with students. Also, remember to participate with them so that you are getting your daily dose of mindfulness too.

Engage Senses

Having students focus on their senses is a great way to practice being more mindful. Whether you bring in food to practice mindful eating together or take them outside to focus on the sound of nature, look for opportunities to engage their senses. When doing these activities use the same principles of awareness you do in your breathing exercises, but transfer this focus to a specific sense.

Guided Meditation

It is often hard to guide mindfulness and teach it at the same time, but thankfully there is an app for that. Actually, there are many apps that you can use in the classroom that will guide you and your students through short mindfulness exercises. For instance, the Calm Schools Initiative sometimes gives free mindfulness training tools to every teacher in the world for free.[84] This gives you access to their paid subscription and even access to their Calm Kids program tailored for students in kindergarten through high school.

Mindful Time-Outs

If you have room, create a space in your classroom that invites students to practice being mindful. Outfit this space with different triggers to help students practice mindfulness. For instance:

- Coloring books (this can be a form of active meditation).
- Device with headphones to listen to white noise, soft music, guided meditations, etc.
- Cue cards with yoga movements and breathing activities
- Tactile basket with stress balls, clay, etc.
- Lava lamps and calming lighting.

When designing this space, make it work for you as well. This will be a great place for you to practice your mindfulness before and after school, on your prep periods or during breaks!

Mindfulness Inquiry

Learn about the importance and effectiveness of being mindful together. Start with an overarching question like, "Is being mindful important in today's world?" From that point on, learn about it, research it, practice it, and reflect on it. Have the students take ownership of learning more about it and finding new ways to practice it together. By making it a year-long inquiry, it will help to keep the momentum going and deepen the learning for everyone involved.

Physical Triggers for Mindfulness

Attaching Meaning to an Object

I have to admit that I find being mindful very difficult; however, one thing that helps me the most is keeping a smooth stone in my pocket. Sounds strange I know, but it works for me. The stone I carry has the word 'Harmony' imprinted on it and was given to me by a dear friend. I use it to help me to remember to be more present. Every time I put my hand in my pocket, it is a reminder that I need to slow down and appreciate the moment.

Obviously, it does not need to be a stone — it could be whatever inanimate object that you attach meaning to. It could be a bracelet, a coffee mug, or student gift that sits on your desk. Have a cue or trigger that you can feel or see. This is a great way to keep you in the moment.

Powerful Password

Try setting your computer passwords to something that helps trigger you to be more mindful. As educators, we are logging into different computers and websites multiple times each day. Look at these logins as an opportunity to remind you to slow down and enjoy the moment. Change your password to reflect your current goals or focus. For instance, use Strive as your password to remind you to focus more on your happiness as an educator (shameless self-promotion!).

Bookend Your Day Being Mindful

Unwind and Refocus

There is a moment each day when the chaos stops, and it becomes quiet again. Your classroom is empty and you are going about your end of the day routines, preparing to go home. Stop, sit and take a moment to breathe, slow down, think, reflect, and be present. Take deep breaths or listen to a song that helps you be present. Take 5 minutes to just stop and take in the moment. Convince yourself that this short amount of time will give you the boost in attention and mood that you need to be productive and enjoy the rest of the evening.

Bedtime Routine

Finish your day the way that you started. Lie in bed, aware of your breath. The day is over, and there is nothing more you are going to do. Clear your thoughts by shifting your awareness back to your breathing and the rise and fall of your chest. This is a great way to unwind. It will help slow your pulse, lower your heart rate and decrease stress hormones, preparing you for a better night's sleep.[85]

Gratitude

As mindfulness increases, so does our ability to practice gratitude. Honing our minds to be able to focus and to become more aware is an essential first step in becoming more grateful.[86] Just as we learned how to focus on our breathing, our senses, and single tasks, we can also learn to be more aware of the aspects of our lives that we are grateful for. Beyond awareness, it is important to acknowledge and develop an appreciation for the positive occurrences in our lives.

There are very strong ties between gratitude and happiness. Studies have shown that around 18.5% of people's happiness could be predicted by the amount of gratitude they experience.[87] In addition, practicing gratitude can be seen as a keystone habit. Studies show that grateful people also:[88]

- Have better relationships.
- Exercise more.
- Experience fewer aches and pains.
- Experience fewer negative emotions.
- Are less aggressive and more empathic.
- Sleep better.
- Have higher self-esteem.

Like mindfulness, educators can build gratitude into both their personal and professional routines. Whether at home or in the classroom, the ideas below can have a significant impact on our overall happiness.

Gratitude Journals

This is the process of recording and reflecting on things that we are grateful for. The idea is that we are rewiring our brain to pick out the positives instead of the negatives. What I like most about gratitude journals is that you can easily customize them to suit you. Whether you are writing in point form or paragraphs, once a week or every day, you will eventually find what works best for you.

Here are some suggestions to help you get the most out of your gratitude journal:

BE SPECIFIC

This is what will make your journal unique and easier to write. For instance, writing broad statements like 'students were great today' will quickly get boring and it will be hard to come up with new things to write. However, if you wrote 'Lauren's big hug at end of day' or 'Reid's top shelf goal in hockey,' it captures a specific moment that you truly are grateful for.

AVOID REPETITION

You do not want this to become something that you do just to do it. It should not be a task, but something that you look forward to. To keep your writing fresh and engaging, try to pull from different domains of your life; home, school, relationships, health, weather, food, etc. This is what will keep it novel and extend the effectiveness of the journal.

WRITE EVEN ON BAD DAYS

Writing in your gratitude journal on a day where everything seemed to go wrong is a great way to practice gratitude. Try to push aside the negatives and find a positive. They are there, you just need to find them.

Building gratitude journals into daily teaching is a great way to help students become more optimistic and grateful. Have students write in individual journals or have a class gratitude journal that you add to each day.

GRATITUDE APP/POST

Personally, I struggle with writing a journal of any kind. My penmanship, or lack of it, has always been a frustration for me. I am very thankful for the rise in the use of technology. When I am typing or texting, I feel fast, efficient, and organized. That is why I love the idea of using an app to journal my gratitude.

I researched many gratitude apps on the market, but my favorite is *Happyfeed*.[89] Each day I get a notification just prior to going to sleep that asked me to write three things that I am grateful for. If I am struggling to think of an idea on those tough days, it will give me hints or prompts. Not only that, I can quickly access my camera roll and add a picture that helps me remember the moment. If you post every day for one year, you would have recognized 1,095 things that you are most grateful for.

As an educator, I can create another account just for teaching. At the end of each day, I could set a notification to remind me to reflect on my day at work and to encourage me to find the positives from my day. This could be something that I share and complete each day with my students, or something that I do just to keep me grateful for the amazing job I am privileged to get to do each day.

My sister used to do something similar to this. At the end of each day, she would post on her class website what she was grateful for that day. She would be very specific; the students could see how much she appreciated them and how grateful she was to be their teacher.

Gratitude Stations

To encourage more gratitude in the classroom or around the school, setting up a gratitude station is a great idea. Outfit this station with thank you cards, stick-it notes, different color markers, stickers, and whatever else you can think of to make expressing gratitude quick and simple.

Locate this station in a high traffic area so that it acts as a trigger to get people thinking about others whom they are grateful for. Also, you can promote gratitude over the announcements to encourage more buy-in from staff and students. Have fun with this, do not be afraid to mix it up once in a while. Perhaps set up different themes or think of prompts that could be added to spark even more gratitude.

Don't forget to participate yourself. By initiating this station, not only are you positively improving the mood of others, but you will find it to have a very positive impact on your overall happiness.

Gratitude Exit Cards

Exit cards are a great way to collect thinking at the end of a class or the day. It is an opportunity to reflect on your learning and experience. Connecting this reflection to gratitude is a great way for both you and your students to close out the day. If you have time, allow students to share what or whom they are grateful for that day. Or this would be a great way to start the following day on a positive note. You could also create a gratitude bulletin board in the room where people can post their gratitude exit cards at the end of the day for others to read. This board becomes symbolic of the many things that happen each day that are positive and that we are grateful for.

TRY NOT TO MISS OUT ON ENJOYING GREAT MOMENTS

MAKE THEM LAST SHARE THEM SAVOUR THEM

SAVORING THE MOMENT

Savoring is a form of mindfulness in which you are focused on prolonging a positive situation. As you notice yourself feeling positive emotions or gratitude, try to extend it by slowing down and enjoying the moment. During these moments, try not to be distracted or move on to the next task too quickly. Take it in. For instance, if a student has an 'aha' moment in class, take the time to enjoy their facial expressions and body language, engage in a conversation about this breakthrough, or celebrate it with them.

One of the best ways to practice savoring is to share it with others. Try to make it a habit to relive the great moments in the day, instead of a bad one. By retelling these stories, you are resurfacing the positive emotions that come along with it. Not only that, the people who you are sharing these moments with leave the conversation feeling more positive and energized.

There are so many great moments that we miss in education because we are too scared to slow down. Make a point of being more aware of these moments and savoring them as much as possible.

MINDFULNESS EXERCISE

1. Sit in a comfortable position with both feet flat on the ground. Keep your back straight, so that your head and neck are in line with your spine. Rest your hands in your lap.

2. Start by focusing on how your body feels. What sensations are you noticing?

3. Move your focus to your breathing. Notice where you feel your breath in your body. It might be in your abdomen, chest, throat or nose.

4. Focus on feeling each breath in and out. Try to maintain focus on only your breathing.

5. It is natural for your mind to wander. When you notice this happening, gently redirect your attention back to your breath.

6. Continue focusing on your breathing for 3-5 minutes.

7. Complete your homework by thinking about a student who brought you great joy. Allow yourself to savor moments that made this student so special to you that they were the one that came into your thoughts. Enjoy this time reminiscing about them.

NOTE

Know that it is very common for your mind to wander often during this exercise. Each time that you are able to redirect your attention back to your breath, you are training your mind to be more aware. The more you practice this, the easier it will be to stay focused and in the moment.

3. POSITIVE INTAKE

"We find whatever it is we're looking for.
Look for the good."
— Al Carraway

How we see the world will have a major impact on how we teach our students and how much we love our jobs. More than ever, our daily routines play an incredible role in programming our brains to focus on either the positive or negative aspects of our lives. These outlooks will affect our happiness, relationships and the impact we will have on others.

Scientists used to believe that the brain did not change beyond childhood. However, over the last decade, science has shown us that the brain continues to change throughout our entire lives. This is due to a process called neuroplasticity.[90]

Essentially, we can rewire our brains through our experiences, repeated behaviors, emotions, and thoughts. Even someone who exudes pessimistic behavior can train themselves to be more optimistic.[91]

The more I work with educators on the topic of happiness in education, the more I realize the influence that perception has on our careers. Often, I see educators who work in the same district or even the same school, with an entirely different perspective on the students they teach, the quality of leadership, and the direction coming from above. This is largely shaped by what their brains are trained to focus on- the positives or the negatives.

We often see this divide between optimists and pessimists on staff. It is remarkably clear the impact that either perspective has on their overall job satisfaction. The good news is that we have the ability to develop a more positive mindset by making changes to our daily routines.

WHY IT IS MORE DIFFICULT TO BE POSITIVE

When I was young, I remember my parents turning on the television at 6pm every night to watch the local news. This was a half hour show that quickly updated them on major world events, local news, sports and weather. If they missed the evening news, they could tune in at noon the next day to catch the afternoon edition.

Times have changed dramatically since then, and so has the way we are consuming media. The habits we have developed around media consumption are taking a major toll on our well-being and outlook on life. The news is a great example. What was once a small part of each day, now runs around the clock on 24-hour news channels. Not only that, we are also constantly bombarded with news through social media and push notifications.

The major issue with this is that the news primarily focuses on the negative. They do so because it is good for ratings and they know that our brains are drawn more to the negative than the positive. This is called a negativity bias. Psychologists believe that our brains are wired this way because our ancestors needed to pay close attention to potentially life-threatening situations that put them in danger. Although intended to keep us safe, it is now training our brains to become more cynical.[92]

To accelerate the issue, we are exposing ourselves to an incredible amount of media each day. For instance, market-research group Nielsen says that in 2018 adults spent, on average, over 11 hours a day interacting with media.[93] Much of this media is intertwined with negative news and content that is having an adverse effect on overall well-being.

How Does Media Affect Happiness

Media can have a positive or negative effect on our overall well-being — it just depends on what type of media we expose ourselves to. For instance, the Harvard Business Review published a study in which participants were exposed to three minutes of either positive or negative media in the morning. Later that day, they completed a survey to assess their overall mood. Those participants who were exposed to negative media had a 27% greater likelihood of reporting their day as unhappy six to eight hours later.[94]

If three minutes of negative media in the morning can have this much impact on our overall happiness, think of the impact that being exposed all day to this media would have. The good news is we control the media that we consume. We control what we watch, what we listen to, and who we follow on social media.

It is imperative that we develop a greater awareness of the impact media is having on our lives. To get an idea, watch the news for an hour and monitor how you feel at the end. More often than not, you will feel negative emotions such as anxiety, fatigue, and frustration. Then try the opposite. Watch something that is positive or inspiring and monitor how this impacts your overall mood. You will find that just exposing yourself to different types of media will have a profound effect on your outlook and happiness.

Replacing the Bad with the Good

A great way to eliminate negative media is to engage in consuming more positive media. Not only are we getting the benefits of eliminating something that is bad for our well-being, we are also getting the benefit of introducing something that is good for us. It is like getting double the dose of happiness.

As educators, we are always busy, and it is often hard to find time to add anything more to our already hectic days. That is why we need to incorporate more joy into our lives by embedding it into things we are already doing. Here are some ways to substitute more positive media into your day.

Audiobooks

Many educators would love to read more, however, they struggle to find the time. That is where audiobooks come in. They can be quickly uploaded on to your device and ready to play in minutes from your device and in your car.

There are many great audiobook apps out there. Once I found out that I could use my library card to access audiobooks, I was hooked. Most libraries are connected to apps such as Overdrive, Libby, and Hoopla. These are free alternatives to purchasing paid audiobook apps. You borrow an audiobook for free like you would a hardcopy book out of the library. Ask your local library for more details.

Podcast

Podcasts are another great option. Essentially, they are shorter interview style audio programs on a wide array of topics. They are easy to access and listen to using a device.

Educational podcasts are the second most listened-to type of podcasts. Research shows that 40% of all podcast listeners tune into education-based talks.[95] If you have not listened to one before, it is worth a try. To find a podcast you like, just Google "educational podcast" and a description of the topic that you would like to hear discussed.

My favorite educational podcast to listen to is *Cult of Pedagogy* with Jennifer Gonzalez.[96] I appreciate the variety of topics she covers and guests she has on the show. It is really easy to listen to a podcast that gives me ideas and insights into different aspects of education. This might be a good place to start if you have never listened to one before.

Playlist

Personally, I find it most beneficial to continuously switch up the types of media I am consuming based on how I am feeling. Usually in between audiobooks, I like to mix in podcasts and music playlists.

I like music playlists because I find them to be an effective way to positively impact my mood. Creating different playlists based on different needs works best for me. For instance, I have a gratitude playlist that helps me focus on the positive aspects of my life. I like to start my day listening to these songs. Then I have a motivation playlist to get me excited enough to exercise. Sometimes I play my 90s Hip Hop playlist when I just want to kick back, have fun and relax. Try making a playlist based on your happy goals, it works!

Taking the time to set up a specific playlist makes it quick and easy to listen to songs you like that are going to have a positive impact on your mood.

Inspirational Videos

Inspirational videos online are a great way to add a positive boost to your day. Taking a short break to watch a video about an inspiring teacher, local hero or a feel good story is sometimes all you need to turn your day around.

One of my guilty pleasures is searching videos from reality TV shows where people audition their talents. I often find their stories very inspiring, and I love watching people in their element and achieving their goals. Just search "best auditions" on YouTube — be careful; it is hard to watch just one!

Although there is a lot of negative content online, if you look, you can find a lot of media that does a great job showing how great people are and the amazing things that we can accomplish if we try hard enough.

Positive Work Environment

As educators, there are a lot of opportunities to not only immerse ourselves in positive content, but to use it to inspire and inform our students.

It is imperative that we teach our students about the importance of regulating their negative media intake and model how positive media can have a significant effect on their well-being.

Here are some examples of how we can build positive media into our day-to-day teaching. In doing this, we are not just positively affecting our students, we are benefitting from it ourselves.

MOTIVATION MONDAYS

What better way to start off the week than with an inspiring video or motivational reading? By committing to this once a week, it does not get overwhelming and gives you lots of time to find the right content to share with the class.

This is a great way to nudge yourself into sourcing out positive content. You will be more focused on the positive when scrolling through social media and browsing websites. This alone will have an impact on your happiness.

Once you find the right video or reading, you will be excited to kick off the week on an inspirational note. Remember as you find these great resources to bookmark them (ctrl + d or command + D on a Mac) in your browser to make them easier to pull up the next time you need a boost!

POSITIVE NEWS WALL

If we know the news teaches our students the world is mostly bad, it is up to us to teach them the truth that a lot of the people in the world are kind, compassionate, and caring. Max Roser from Oxford University's Institute for Economic Thinking shows through his research that the world is actually safer than ever. He states, "We live in a much more peaceful and inclusive world than our ancestors of the past."[97]

Creating a Positive News Wall in your classroom is a great way to highlight and celebrate the great things that are happening around the world, in your community, and in your school. Designate a bulletin board in your classroom as a place where you and your students can post positive news. Challenge them to be on the lookout for articles and news posts on local heroes, philanthropists and other inspiring people.

By making this a physical space in your classroom, it acts as a reminder to focus more on the positive than the negative. It will also hopefully inspire them to make positive changes in their lives and the lives of others.

POSITIVE MEDIA LITERACY UNIT

Media literacy is becoming more and more of a hot topic in education since "Fake News" has become a thing, for lack of better words. It is our responsibility to teach our students how to interpret and filter media effectively.

Part of this is teaching them why making healthier choices with regard to media consumption matters. We must ensure they realize how negative media can skew their perceptions of the world and train their brains to become more pessimistic.

It would be interesting to integrate Media Literacy and Health into a unit that gives students the tools to select media that will help improve well-being. As educators, planning and teaching this unit would help keep this at the forefront of our minds.

MEET A HERO

There are some truly inspiring people in the world who give selflessly to make the world a better place. These are the people that we want our students to look up to. Making everyday heroes a class focus is an inspiring way to bring more positivity into your class.

I met a teacher who was telling me about a hero unit he was working on. During his planning, he discovered that CNN Heroes was a great place to learn about everyday people doing extraordinary things to change the world. He said his students loved it, and this inspired him to take it even deeper. He contacted some of the CNN heroes and was able to set up a Skype conversation with his class. This was an incredible way to inspire his class in a powerful and authentic way.

Being creative about how to introduce yourself and your students to inspiring people is a great way to promote positivity and to create future heroes.

POSITIVE INTAKE BEYOND MEDIA

To extend the idea of positive intake further, look for other ways to invest more time focusing on the positive and less time on the negative. The more we build this into our daily routines, the happier we will be. Here are some more ideas on ways to invest energy on the many great aspects of education.

TEACHER TREASURE CHEST

Every teacher has days that do not go well. Sometimes entire weeks do not go well! In times like these, it is nice to have a teacher treasure chest of memories, notes of appreciation, photographs, and

THE WORLD WILL SEEM LIKE A MUCH **BETTER PLACE**

IF YOU TRAIN YOUR BRAIN TO PICK OUT THE POSITIVES

any other artifacts that make you smile. Spending a couple of minutes focusing on the positive memories is a great way to pull you out of a negative slump.

If you do not like clutter, you can make a digital version that you can easily access on your computer. If you can get in the habit of taking pictures of artifacts that mean a lot to you, you can store them online and have access to them anywhere, anytime.

As parents, my wife and I have started to do this with a lot of our own kid's schoolwork. It is hard to throw it out, but we need to. So now we take pictures of it and then discreetly put it in the garbage.

Personal Teaching Wall of Fame

Some artifacts are just too important to store away in a chest or online. They belong somewhere that you can see them daily as a reminder of the difference you are making each day. They deserve to be on your teacher wall of fame.

I am fortunate to have had the opportunity to be in hundreds of different classrooms. I really enjoy when teachers create a collage of student notes, class pictures, and inside jokes behind their desk. It is a great way to make the positive aspects of the job prevalent in your mind. When you are stressed, tired ,or battling negativity, you can just swing your chair around and be reminded of why you love to teach.

Positivity Policy

A policy is a plan that is used as a basis for making decisions to help one achieve a specific outcome.[98]

Creating a Positivity Policy involves cutting out as much negativity as possible, and replacing it with positivity. That means that you try to engage in fewer negative conversations with other staff members, focus more on student strengths than weaknesses, and concentrate on the great aspects of the profession.

If you can implement and work toward your Positivity Policy, it will eventually develop into a habit. That means it will become more natural and automatic. You will get better at finding the positives and avoiding the negatives.

Train Your Brain

We are fortunate that our brains have the ability to be trained, just like our muscles. To be happy, we need to analyze what we consume mentally on a daily basis. Finding ways to absorb more positive messages throughout the day will have a significant impact on how we see the world and our happiness.

1. Reflect on your positive and negative intake by completing
    the table below. Start by thinking about your media]
    consumption and relationships.

NEGATIVE INTAKE	POSITIVE INTAKE

2. From the negative intake side, select one or two that you
    could easily replace with something more positive.

3. As you replace something negative with a positive, make sure
    to reflect on how it affects your mood and overall outlook.

4. SOCIALIZATION

"Individually, we are one drop.
Together, we are an ocean."
— *Ryunosuke Satoro*

The healthiest, happiest, and oldest people on the planet have shown us that the quantity and quality of our social interactions are pivotal to our well-being. The more research that is collected on the six Blue Zone communities, the more we realize the impact face to face interactions have on our lives. The Blue Zone's Team of researchers state that our daily live interactions are, "one of the strongest predictors of how long you'll live." [99]

Another meta-analysis study out of Brigham Young University looked at how loneliness impacted the life expectancy of over three million people. Their findings suggest that being lonely, "represents a greater health risk than obesity and is as destructive to your health as smoking 15 cigarettes a day." Additionally, they found that loneliness can increase mortality risk by up to 32% and reduce life by up to eight years. [100]

Fortunately for educators, the design of our current education system is an ideal environment to connect daily with different people on different levels. Understanding the value that these interactions have on our overall health and happiness is key to ensuring that we make getting to know staff and students a top priority. The frequency and way in which we socialize to be happier depends on our personality, outgoingness, and comfort level.

IDEAL CONDITIONS FOR SOCIALIZATION

The village of Villagrande is said to be the epicenter of Sardinia's Blue Zone. It is the only place in the world that men live as long as women. Researchers believe that traditionally women live longer than men because they "prioritize and groom their face to face relationships better over their lifetime." However, in Villagrande, both sexes equally make socialization a priority and both reap the benefits of longevity and health. [101]

In Susan Pinker's TED talk, *The Secrets to Living Longer,* she describes how the density and 'interwoven' streets in villages such as Villagrande nudge those who live there to socialize more. It is this constant stream of interactions that contribute to Sardinia having ten times more centenarians than North America. [102]

One commonality of the happiest people in the world is that they spend, on average, five to six hours a day socializing face-to-face. Just to

put this in perspective, North Americans spend, on average, 41 minutes a day socializing in person.[103] This increase in real socialization is important because it helps release the feel-good hormones such as; oxytocin and serotonin. Not only do these hormones positively affect your mood, they also help to reduce stress and build positive relationships.[104]

Similar to Blue Zones, schools are densely populated communities of interdependent people. Our classrooms and hallways connect us and give us the opportunity to engage in meaningful face to face interactions throughout the majority of our day. We must try to invest time and energy into fostering relationships with not only our students, but also with those we work with.

Those Who Play Together, Stay Together

If it is all work and no play, then we are missing out on a vital aspect of loving our jobs. Going to work should not be something that we dread. If it is, we need to make some changes.

A great place to start is to inject some fun into our day by setting aside time for play. Of course, this would not be fun alone. Find someone or a group of people who, like you, are in need of a little mental break and a few laughs.

If you ask students what they love most about school, one of the more popular answers would be extracurriculars. For many students, this is what makes them want to come to school each day. It is a break from the work they do in the classroom, and it is an opportunity to interact with their peers on a different level and in a different context. We recognize the importance of this for our students, now we need to recognize its importance for staff.

Teacher Clubs

One of the most common ways to start a club in school is to post a sign up sheet and see who is interested. As educators, we can use this same strategy. In the staffroom, create a space where educators can sign up for clubs specifically designed for them. It might surprise you how many people will sign up.

I was talking to a high school teacher who set up a CrossFit gym at his school. He was very passionate about this space and added to it every year. Eventually, he decided to offer his staff the opportunity to take part in Boot Camps after school. Of the 48 educators on staff, 27 come to his after school classes.

Beyond improving their fitness levels and emotional well-being, it is helping to bring the staff together to socialize and form friendships. It is also very convenient for teachers to have a quick work out after school, so that they can focus on their family, passions, or other obligations in the evenings.

Remember that this club does not need to be limited to your staff. I met another teacher who had a passion for singing. After discussing the importance of chasing our passions in a workshop, she posted online that her dream was to have drop-in choir club for educators across our district. Within hours, other educators expressed their interest and support. With a little perseverance, this dream will become a reality.

Creating a Teacher Club starts with being vulnerable enough to take the risk. You might not get everyone on board that you would like, however, the people you do get, will likely be the ones that will form into those meaningful friendships that you are looking for. Now just like the students, you will have a little something extra to look forward to during your school day.

Educator Outings

I have the opportunity to spend a lot of time with educators outside of school hours. The one thing about them is that they love to have fun when they get together. They are usually the loudest and most entertaining group in the establishment. However, most staff tend to only socialize as a group a couple of times throughout the year.

Many schools have started planning class trips earlier in the year. The logic is that the time outside of school will bring the entire group closer together. Interacting in a different environment has the potential to create new connections within the group.

I often witnessed this as a grade eight teacher. We would do a three-day overnight graduation trip at the end of the year. On the bus ride home, you could feel a noticeable change in group dynamics. I recall always thinking that we should have done it sooner.

Finding appropriate outings for a staff gathering is a great way to foster relationship building on staff. You can use the same strategy as starting a Teacher Club. Just post in the staffroom an idea for a night out and see what happens. Often, we wait for our administration to initiate these events. However, if you are looking to have more fun at work and want to get to know the staff better, take the risk and see what happens.

Work Dates

If you talk to a relationship therapist, they will tell you that you need to book 'Date Nights.' They feel that this is important because it shows that you are making your relationship a priority. By committing your time to someone, it demonstrates that you value their company.

The life of an educator is a busy one. Often, we get so busy that we forget to stop and spend time with others on staff that we enjoy. This might get us slightly ahead in the workload department; however, it depletes us in other areas. One of those areas is the culturing of relationships into friendship. In order to tap into more happiness at work, this is something that we need to make a priority.

I love the idea of setting up scheduled work dates with people you enjoy. Perhaps you commit a specific break or planning period each week to spend together. The key is to write this in your day book, just like you would an appointment. Honor this time and commit to being present. By making this commitment and honoring it, you are telling that person that you enjoy their company and would like to continue to build on the friendship.

Book Clubs

Book clubs are a great way to promote more socialization on staff, while at the same time shifting the school culture in the right direction. Committing to a book club also nudges us into making reading a priority, as we know that others are counting on us.

When selecting a book to read as a staff, try to find something that will inspire and unite the staff together. Your hope is that the book engages staff members in meaningful conversations that will deepen relationships and help them grow as educators.

Remember, select the right time of year to start a book club. Avoid report card season and heavy marking months. If you feel that everyone is too busy, try running a book club over the summer. It is a great way to nudge staff to get together on their months off. This will help build on the momentum of relationship development that you have been working on throughout the year.

It is best to meet in person; however, if you cannot, technology makes book clubs easier than ever. You can set up something simple like a group text chat or explore a more advanced platform like video conferencing. There are many tools online now that are easy to set up and that you can use to help you meet virtually.

Team TV Watching

If we are going to invest time in watching TV, we might as well make it a team effort. I get the opportunity to sit in many different staff rooms. The ones that stand out as the most fun are the ones that are debating over which character will be kicked off the island, which team will win the Stanley Cup, or who will be chosen for an Oscar.

Setting up a pool based on a TV show or sporting tournament is a fun way to get the staff laughing and joking. Making it visual in the staff room helps people connect, discussing who each person has picked and nudging people into initiating conversations with people they might not normally interact with. If you get a good uptake in your pool and everyone is enjoying it, this sets you up perfectly for a group outing to watch the final episode or game.

Some staff need to relax and play more together. Setting up something like this promotes taking time out of our busy schedules to joke around and socialize on a different level. It only takes one person to initiate turning random TV-watching into something that brings the staff together to generate a lot of laughs throughout the day.

Professional Friendship Development

Most of my TFFs (Teacher Friends Forever) stem from having the opportunity to work together in the classroom. There is something special about learning, planning, and pushing each other to improve as educators. The more we have the opportunity to work together, the more layers we see of each other's personality, and the more we appreciate each other's talents and passions.

Collaboration is necessary if we want to grow in this profession. The key is to seek out opportunities that enable us to work side by side with other educators. Whether that be in staff meetings, learning teams, or self-initiated professional development, we must find educators that will push our thinking.

Co-Teaching

The old adage, "Two heads are better than one," holds true in education. Connecting with another teacher or group of teachers to plan a unit or lesson is great on so many levels. From my experiences, the final product that is delivered to students is always much superior than if I were to have created the lesson/unit in isolation.

Try to flow between learner and leader in these settings. When we can achieve this balance, we cultivate an environment that promotes mutual respect and trust. This lays the foundations for future friendships and great experiences inside and outside of the classroom.

In my fourth year of teaching, I changed schools and was introduced to my new teaching partner. Melissa was very quiet and reserved, while I was young and overly energetic. I recall our first real conversation when I told her I had all sorts of great resources that she could use. I was not looking to see what I could learn from her, I just assumed that she would want my help. Little did I know, she was a pedagogical genius.

We worked in silos for the first couple of years. In our third year as teaching partners, we agreed to work together on a novel study. By that point, my ego had diminished slightly, and I was able to assume the role of learner. For lack of better terms, it was mind-blowing to me the manner in which she scaffolded learning for her students. Her ability to select the appropriate strategies and her insights into assessment were all areas that I needed to improve.

She developed an appreciation for my creativity, work ethic, and use of technology. Very quickly, we learned that this union of teaching styles would result in a powerful and unique experience for our students. We collaborated through the entire unit, then never stopped. Even as our careers went in different directions, we found ways to work together and to spend time together. She is now one of my best friends and someone that I consider to be the most powerful influence in my teaching career.

Beyond the lessons and learning, it brought new excitement to our day-to-day teaching. Having someone to collaborate with is fun. We looked forward to delivering lessons together and shared many laughs along the way. We also developed deeper personal and professional respect for each other, and following that, a great friendship.

MENTORING

One of the aspects of teaching that I find most fulfilling is being an associate teacher to future teaching candidates. For the most part, they are so raw and eager to learn. I love watching their growth in confidence from day one until the end of their teaching assignment. There is something very satisfying about passing on your knowledge and expertise.

THERE COMES A POINT IN YOUR CAREER WHERE IT IS

YOUR TURN TO GIVE BACK

OFTEN BEING A **MENTOR** IS AS REWARDING AS BEING MENTORED

Similar to collaborating with another staff member, there is the potential for special relationships to form between mentor and mentee. I still keep in contact with many of the student teachers I have worked with over the years. Some have become great friends and people I still collaborate with. One in particular has become a major part of my life.

I met Mike on the first day of his first teaching internship. He was assigned as a student teacher for my class. We worked together every day for three weeks. He was phenomenal at taking constructive feedback. Every day I saw a remarkable improvement from the day before, it was incredible to watch. By week three, he was an awesome teacher. I was so proud.

After this teaching assignment was over, we kept in touch. Randomly, he ended up living in my basement for three months as he got a teaching job in our district and did not have a place to live. Over the past decade, we have become amazing friends, so much so that I was the best man at his wedding ten years later. As I reflect on this journey from associate teacher to best man, I think it has a lot to do with those three weeks working side by side and the bond that was created.

As we advance in our teaching careers, it is only right that we give back to the profession. The best way to do this is to take another teacher under our wing — help them to be successful and share with them the knowledge that we have developed over the years. Mentorship is a win-win situation for everyone involved. It can provide more opportunities for personal growth, which can also be more meaningful and improve social interactions.

FIND YOUR SOCIAL NICHE ON STAFF

Regardless if you are a social butterfly on staff who loves to organize events or someone who prefers to invest in more intimate connections, try to find your social niche on staff. Make your niche one that helps you feel connected, supported, and that brings fun into each day. Find a way to build making time for others into your daily routines and work life. It is these relationships that you foster that will have perhaps the greatest impact on your overall happiness, resilience, and professional growth.

1. Place a dot on the scale below that represents the amount of
    meaningful face to face social interactions you have with staff

    ├───┤
    Low   High

2. Place a dot on the scale below that represents the amount of
    meaningful social interaction you have with staff outside of the
    school day.

    ├───┤
    Low   High

3. Brainstorm different ways that could increase the amount of
    meaningful interactions you have with your staff.

4. Pick one way to increase your interaction with your staff and
    organize something fun to do together.

5. SIGNATURE STRENGTHS & SKILLS

"The good life consists of deriving happiness
by using your signature strengths every day."
— Martin Seligman

If you were to analyze each working day, how much of that time are you using your strengths? In this context, strength refers to things that you are naturally good at. This is a good question to ask because it has a direct impact on your happiness at work. The research shows that people who use their strengths daily are six times more likely to be engaged. Not only that, they also are more productive and less likely to want to leave their jobs.[105]

As educators, it is valuable for us to develop an awareness of our strengths and how much we use them. This knowledge can be used to help guide our career paths and find more joy in our day-to-day work life. The greater our self-awareness with regard to these strengths, the more likely it is that we will use them to their full potential.

Dr. Lea Waters, president of the International Positive Psychology Association and author of the book Strength Switch, promotes the idea that we should be building on strengths rather than focusing on weaknesses. This can help build, "optimism, resilience and achievement."[106]

SURVEYING YOUR STRENGTHS

Often it can be difficult to accurately assess our own strengths. That is why we must rely on others to help us with this. People around us get a unique view of our strengths that we might not see. Often, we focus too much on areas we need to improve, and not enough on strengths that we can build on.

When you ask someone to help identify your strengths, explain to them why it is important to you. This is not about an ego boost or a pep talk, this is about tapping into these areas more as an educator. Encourage them to be honest and give examples if possible. Take time to write down their observations, so that you can refer to them when needed.

Try to get multiple perspectives. Ask a family member, a friend outside of education, a colleague at work, and your administration. They all see you through different lenses and might give you different insights into your strengths.

An amazing way to self-assess your strengths is by completing the VIA Character Strength Profile.[107] This is a free online survey that takes less than

KNOWING WHERE OUR **STRENGTHS** LIE CAN NOT ONLY MAKE US BETTER EDUCATORS

IT CAN ALSO MAKE US **HAPPIER**

15 minutes to complete. It is scientifically validated, private and confidential. It was created by Martin Seligman, the father of Positive Psychology.

Upon completion of the survey, the VIA institute will rank your 24 Character Strengths from greatest to least. Here is a list of the strengths that are measured on this survey. They are organized under core virtues.[108]

WISDOM	TEMPERANCE
Creativity	Forgiveness
Curiosity	Humility
Judgment	Prudence
Perspective	Self-Regulation
Love of Learning	
TRANSCENDENCE	**JUSTICE**
Appreciation of Beauty	Fairness
Gratitude	Leadership
Hope	Teamwork
Humor	
Spirituality	
COURAGE	**HUMANITY**
Bravery	Kindness
Honesty	Love
Perseverance	Social Intelligence
Zest	

It is worth mentioning that everyone has all 24 strengths, just in different amounts. Those you use less should not be seen as a weakness, these are strengths that come less naturally to you and require more effort to use.

I showed my wife my results and she totally agreed with how they ranked my character strengths. She said it was a great representation of where my strengths lie. I like to go back to this survey when I am considering changing or taking on new initiatives. I find it helps ensure that I take on roles that will fit nicely with my strengths and gives me confidence moving forward.

SIGNATURE SKILLS

Our strengths may come naturally to us, but our skills are developed through practice and effort. Both can have a significant impact on our happiness at work. Like strengths, we need to utilize our skills in our daily practice. We have invested time and energy into developing these skills because we feel they are valuable, and we are drawn to them.

It is amazing to watch a teacher bring their guitar into class to spice up a lesson. We may not all have skills that make us look this cool, but we do have skills that could bring us this level of enjoyment. By investing in skills we are passionate about and finding ways to use them to teach, we experience many benefits that will enhance our teaching practice and help us love our jobs more.

For me, it was Photoshop. I loved how you could manipulate images and create amazing things using this product. Eventually, I discovered that our district had a license to this program and that we could install it on every computer. I began to look for new ways to build this into my lessons. The students loved it and each time we used it in class, I felt a boost of excitement and happiness.

My love of Photoshop developed into a love of using technology to inspire students to learn. The more I invested into this skill, the more opportunities presented themselves. Eventually, I started teaching technology to other classes, then to other teachers on staff, and this led to a role as a technology consultant.

If we develop a skill and find a way to effectively and consistently utilize it in the classroom, it can become a signature skill. This is a skill that you are known for and that becomes a unique part of your teaching style. Once you have established this signature skill, more opportunities will present themselves. This will allow you to do more of what you love to do at work.

Developing Your Signature Skills

Brainstorm Your Skills

Make a list of things that you enjoy doing and would like to do more of if you had the time. Analyze this list to see which of these passions could be brought into the classroom or school culture. It does not have to connect to lessons, it could also be an extracurricular activity for staff and/or students.

Start Small and Analyze

Take a risk and incorporate one of these skills into your teaching practice. Remember that sometimes it takes time for things to stick and that at the beginning is always the toughest. Continually analyze if utilizing this skill is having a positive impact on you and your students.

INVEST MORE

If you see that this skill is having a positive impact, look to invest more time into it. Whether that means incorporating it more during lessons, teaching others, or furthering your own learning, invest time and energy into it. If it is something you really enjoy, take an additional qualification course and officially add this skill to your portfolio. The more opportunities that you embrace, the greater the development of this signature skill.

CHALLENGE YOURSELF

Developing your signature skills requires you to continually challenge yourself. Introducing these skills to students is a great way to continue your learning. Engaged students are great at asking questions and constantly pushing learning forward. Empower them to learn beyond what you know. It will advance skill levels of both you and your students.

FLOW AND HAPPINESS

The term flow in psychology refers to the feeling we get when we are fully immersed in an activity that we enjoy and that challenges our strengths/skills. It is identified by what feels like a loss of time or feeling that we are in the 'zone.'

If a task is too difficult and we do not have adequate skills, the result will be stress. If a task is too easy and requires a low level of skills, the result will be apathy and boredom. Neither are good when it comes to experiencing more joy.

The research of Mihaly Csikszentmihalyi, founder of the term flow in this context, revealed that people are happiest when they are fully absorbed in an activity that challenges them. [109]

Flow becomes very important in education in relation to our growth as educators. At the beginning, teaching can be very stressful as we have not yet developed the skills we need to be successful in many areas. However, as we learn these skills, we need to ensure that we continually look to find new ways to challenge ourselves. Our happiness in the profession depends on it.

UNDERSTANDING AND ACHIEVING FLOW

Try to think of an experience in your life when time flew by while doing something that you love to do; a time where everything seemed effortless, yet fulfilling. This is flow.

Mihaly Csikszentmihalyi states that there are eight characteristics that identify if a person is in a state of flow. These are:[110]

1. Complete concentration on a task;
2. A clear goal and immediate feedback;
3. Feeling that time went quickly;
4. Experience is intrinsically rewarding;
5. Feels effortless;
6. Balance between the challenge and your skill;
7. Loss of self-conscious rumination;
8. Feeling of control over the task.

Achieving a state of flow is not a rare event that only artists, poets and athletes experience. It is a state of engagement that you can experience often if you create the right conditions. Here are seven key steps to finding flow:

- Pick something that you are passionate about. Flow starts with intrinsic motivation.

- Set goals. This helps you recognize the challenges involved in reaching the goal.

- Refine skills that will help you achieve your goal.

- Use feedback to adjust your goals. As skill increases, increase the challenge.

- Avoid distractions. To stay in flow, you must stay engaged on the task at hand.

- Build into your routines. Engaging regularly in flow activities helps you build this skill set and make progress.

- Remind yourself it is about the process, not the final product. Just enjoy being engaged in an activity that you like and that challenges you.

BUILDING FLOW INTO YOUR EVERYDAY

As educators, there are many ways that we can achieve flow through our work. We just need to look for those opportunities where our skill level is met by the challenges at hand. We need to actively embrace our passion, skills, and strengths more often throughout the day. Here are some great ways to help you add more flow to your day.

COACHING

Getting involved in coaching is a great way to utilize those skills that you have developed throughout the years. Constantly pushing yourself to come up with new ways to get the most out of your team is a great way to achieve flow. Often you will hear coaches and athletes comment on how quickly the season flew by. This is because they were actively engaged in getting better at something they are passionate about.

CLUBS

Running a club at school is a great way to tap deeper into your passions and interests. By committing to a club, you are ensuring that you spend more time doing something you are passionate about. Remember clubs are not just about supervision, get in there and work alongside the students. It is a great way to use those character strengths we talked about earlier.

LESSONS

Design lessons around subjects that you are passionate about. Push yourself to make these lessons more meaningful and engaging for your students. Whether this be how you deliver the lesson, the activities you create, or the assessment you select, challenge yourself. Go into these lessons excited to teach them and aim to make the time fly by for both you and your students.

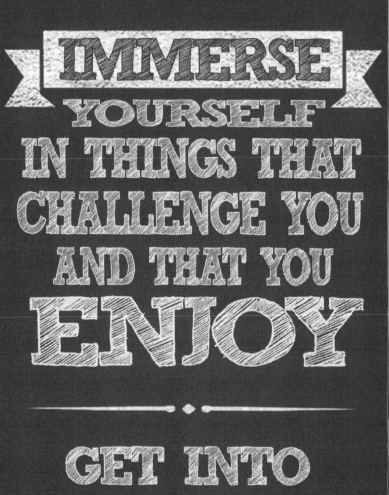

Leadership

Leading others can be very difficult, but also very engaging. If you enjoy leadership and it matches up with your character strengths, this might be a great opportunity to add more flow to your day. It is important to note that leadership does not necessarily mean administration. There are many opportunities to become a leader in a school. If you can connect a passion you have with leadership, it can have a very positive impact on both you and the school.

Volunteering

Committing your time to volunteering and making a difference is a great way to add engagement to your day. It opens up the opportunity for you to use your character strengths and skills in a way that is meaningful and fulfilling. Try to find the right role for you when volunteering. Focus your energy on pushing yourself to improve in areas that you enjoy. Too often we find ourselves in roles that do not allow us to challenge ourselves in a way that makes our involvement exciting and engaging.

Leisure Activities

Making time each week to participate in an activity you enjoy is a great way to build in flow and help you detach from work. Join a club, get a membership, take lessons, find a group of friends who love what you do, and commit to developing a skill along with them. When you are comfortable, try to incorporate what you have learned or the skills you have developed into your teaching practice.

Teaching Using the Idea of Flow

Self-reflecting on our strengths, skills, and passions can make us better educators. What we learn about ourselves, we can pass on to our students. Deepening our learning on the ideas of flow and engagement can lead to philosophical changes in how we teach our students and the assignments we have them do.

When teaching, ensure that the students' skill levels are challenged appropriately. If the assignment is too easy, they will be bored. If the assignment is too challenging, they will be stressed. Using the concept of flow, we want to find a middle ground where each student is challenged and engaged.

When setting up assignments, consider these ideas that increase the chance of students achieving flow:

EMBRACE STUDENT CHOICE

In order for students to be highly engaged in a task, they need to have control over learning. The more control they have over the topic or the final product, the more likely they are to find flow. That is why Genius Hour is so successful. Students use their strengths, skills, and passions to drive their learning. Often in assignments like this, students go well beyond the expectations of both time on task and effort.

TAP INTO INTRINSIC MOTIVATION

Intrinsic motivation is key to entering the state of flow. The goal is to create a shift in why students are working on the assignment. It needs to go from doing something for the teacher to doing it for themselves. Designing tasks that are engaging and that meet their skill levels are critical components for a transference of motivation to occur. The more you know your students, the more likely this is to happen.

PROVIDE SCAFFOLDING

We must support our students through this process. If we give students a task that is overwhelming and too difficult, they will get frustrated and lose engagement. However, if we break down the assignments to match their skill level, they will build confidence and increase engagement. The more cognizant we are about their level of skill and the challenge we give them, the more likely they are to stay engaged and enjoy the task.

MINIMIZE DISTRACTIONS

This can be a tough one to control. However, when students are engaged, they are more on task. By selecting the right assignment that will engage and push them at the right intensity, you can create a learning environment that allows them to stay focused and on task. Try to set up the class so they have blocks of time to work uninterrupted. If you only give them 15 minutes at the end of class, they will not have time to get into flow.

HELP STUDENTS MONITOR PROGRESS

Teach students how to set goals and monitor their own progress. Learning to set short term goals and work toward them will help maintain their level of engagement. We can support students by encouraging self-reflection. Feedback is an essential part of achieving flow. It helps students pace their learning and keeps them in the zone.

This Book is a Result of Flow

Often people will ask me where I found the time to write this book while teaching full time. I try to explain to them that I never looked at this book as extra work. It was my way of finding flow and engagement in every day. Often, I would be so engaged in writing that hours would pass, and it felt like minutes. I began to love this feeling and realized that writing this book has brought me a lot of happiness.

Finding ways to align our signature skills and strengths with our passions will help us engage in flow. The more we can engage in flow, the more effortless and fulfilling life and education become.

1. In the box below, make a list of signature skills that you have developed throughout your life. Highlight the signature skills that you could bring into your teaching practice to make school more engaging for you and your students.

2. Highlight the strengths below that you feel come most naturally to you.

Creativity	Forgiveness	Appreciation of Beauty
Curiosity	Humility	Gratitude
Judgment	Prudence	Hope
Perspective	Self-Regulation	Humour
Love of Learning	Bravery	Spirituality
Fairness	Honesty	Kindness
Leadership	Perseverance	Love
Teamwork	Zest	Social Intelligence

3. Go to www.viacharacter.org and click on "Take Free Survey".

4. Complete the VIA Character Strength Profile online and compare your results with the strengths that you have highlighted above. Reflect on which of the signature strengths you are using daily.

6. KINDNESS

"Be kind whenever possible. It is always possible."
— Dalai Lama

If you want to be happy, be kind. This is an amazing lesson to teach our students. It is also an amazing way to live our lives. Building acts of kindness into our daily routines will have a powerful ripple effect on not only our happiness, but the happiness of everyone around us.

There is strong research to suggest that performing an act of kindness produces the "most reliable momentary increase in well-being."[111] When an act of kindness is committed or even witnessed, our bodies experience a surge of hormones that improve our mood and have a positive impact on our overall health. Three of the hormones that have a significant effect on our mood are often referred to as the Happiness Trifecta.

> **Oxytocin.** Often called the "love hormone." It helps to create intimacy, trust and build healthy relationships. It has also been proven to reduce blood pressure, cardiovascular stress, and improve the immune system.[112]

> **Serotonin.** This is a hormone that helps to regulate mood, social behavior, appetite, digestion, sleep and memory. Recent studies indicate that serotonin impacts the speed in which we learn new information.[113]

> **Dopamine.** This is the feel-good hormone responsible for giving us that feeling of euphoria. It plays a significant role in our motivation, concentration and our ability to persevere.[114]

When you consider the positive impact that these three hormones have on our mood and well-being, you can only imagine the impact this will have on student learning and motivation. Likewise, we, as educators, will get the same positive impact on our day. Being kind throughout each day is an amazing way to regulate your mood and make every day more enjoyable.

Beyond the immediate, short term boost in happiness, building acts of kindness into your daily routines has been shown to have many positive long-term effects. For instance, people who volunteer for two or more

MAKE BEING **KIND** A PERSONAL GOAL A CLASS GOAL A SCHOOL GOAL

THERE CAN NEVER BE ENOUGH KINDNESS IN THE WORLD

organizations in retirement have a 44% less likelihood of dying early.[115] Additionally, Harvard research has shown that those who are altruistic are the happiest. When you invest in being kind, you are also investing in being happier and healthier.[116]

KINDNESS IS TEACHABLE

As educators, we know that almost anything can be a teachable moment. But kindness is much more than just a quick lesson. Dr. Ritchie Davidson compares kindness to weight training. He states, "people can actually build up their compassion 'muscle' and respond to others' suffering with care and desire to help."[117]

The key is consistency! Our students need to see kindness and experience kindness regularly if we want them to be kind. We need to create a culture within our classroom and school where kindness is cool. Whether we are formally building this into our lessons or modeling it throughout our daily interactions with staff and students, they need to see it.

By investing in kindness, not only are students going to be happier coming to school, research suggests it will increase peer acceptance and emotional well-being.[118] Sadly, empathy in students is on the decline. Studies have shown that there has been a 40% decline in student empathy over a 10-year period.[119] To combat this trend, we need to make being kind to others a key component of the soft skills we teach our students.

Don't stop with teaching just your class to be kind. Make it your goal to spread kindness throughout the entire school, staff, and community. Here are some great ideas on ways you can start spreading kindness at your school.

KINDNESS AS A CLASS

Building kindness into your classroom routines is a great way to make sure students consistently experience positive effects on their mood. Here is a list of ideas that you could try with your class:

CHOOSE KIND

Inspired by the book Wonder, the Choose Kind Campaign is a great way to promote kindness. As a class, you can pledge to Choose Kind and even become a Certified Kind Classroom. Each of these classes receives an exclusive Choose Kind Banner and are entered into win some amazing prizes. To learn more, go to:

www.wonderthebook.com/choose-kind

Kindness Snowball Fight

Looking to spice things up a little? Give each student a white piece of paper and ask them to write something kind about someone on it. Have them crumple it into a ball. Set a timer for a short duration of time. Have students throw the crumpled paper balls ("snowballs") around the room until the alarm sounds. Then have students pick up one of the snowballs around them and read it aloud. This is a fun way to get students to share kind thoughts with each other.

Kindness Class Code

Create a kindness code with your class. Have students pledge to follow this code inside and outside of the classroom. Each morning, recite this code together. By starting your day like this, you are building it into the culture of your class and starting each day with kindness in mind. If you want to take it even further, after you pledge, read a kindness quote together. To make it easy on you, google Random Acts of Kindness quotes- they are incredible.

Kindness Calendar

Like Kindness bingo cards, you can find premade calendars online or you can make your own as a class. Each day, an act of kindness is performed either as an individual or a group. This is a great way to ensure you are building kindness into every school day. On the Random Act of Kindness website, you will find a Kindness calendar for every month. This way you can jump right into your kindness calendar at any point in the year!

 www.randomactsofkindness.org/printables

Be Kind Online

The students we teach spend a lot of time online. Unfortunately, this can be a space that can be very unkind. As educators, we should encourage and teach students that being kind online is important. If your students come up with a great idea about how to promote more kindness online, have them submit a grant proposal to the website below.

 www.bekindonline.com

KINDNESS BINGO

A fun way to promote more kindness as a class is bingo! You can find many premade kindness bingo cards online, or you can use an online bingo card generator. They are quick, easy to make, and can be printed from your computer. If you want to get the students more involved in the process, create a kindness bingo card as a class or have them each create their own and share it.

KINDNESS AS A SCHOOL

Once you see the positive impact that kindness will have on your students, look to spread more. You can use your students as your kindness leaders or start a kindness club with students from all grades. Here are some great ideas on how some schools are promoting kindness in their buildings.

BUDDY BENCH

A buddy bench is a special bench where students can sit at recess to let others know that they are looking for someone to play with, they want to make new friends or they are interested in playing something different. Look up Buddy Benches online or try to find a community member who is willing to donate their time to design one for your school. These have been popping up more and more in my district, and it is having a positive impact on nudging students to be kinder and more inclusive on the playground

THIRD-PARTY COMPLIMENT

Encourage your Kindness Team to collect written compliments directed at either staff or students. Have a Kindness Team member deliver these compliments to the person they were written about and have them read it out loud. To amplify the effect, record each person reading the third party compliments they received. Once you have enough, edit these clips together into an inspiring video and share with others. To see the impact these have on students, search Third Party Compliments on Youtube!

DECORATE WITH KINDNESS

Sometimes all we need to be kind is a simple reminder. I love going into schools that use kindness as decor. Here are some ideas that I have seen and loved:

- Kindness quotes on stairs
- Bathroom stalls painted with inspiring messages
- Bulletin boards celebrating and promoting Random Acts of Kindness
- Caught being kind slips
- Kindness paper chains lining hallways
- Rocks painted with kindness quotes in rock garden
- Positive chalk art on tarmac

THE GREAT KINDNESS CHALLENGE

Looking for an easy way to get the entire school practicing kindness, sign up for the Great Kindness Challenge. Each student receives a checklist with 50 acts of kindness they need to complete in one week. So far, 13 million students worldwide have committed 650 million acts of kindness through this challenge. Check out their website to see the incredible impact this is having on school culture.

www.thegreatkindnesschallenge.com

KIND IN THE COMMUNITY

As a school, decide on a way to give back to the community. Rally the school around helping others. Some ideas that I have seen that worked really well were:

- Fun Fair where proceeds go to a local charity
- Clothing drive to help families in need
- Be Kind to your Neighbor event
- Kindness Spirit Days

KINDNESS ON STAFF

Students look up to their teachers. They are constantly learning from us. Not just through our lessons, but also by our actions. It is powerful when educators model kindness with their peers and allow students to witness it. This will have a positive impact on both students and teachers, and it will help to build those strong relationships needed at work. Here are some fun ways that you can spread a little kindness to those you work with:

- Sneak into another teacher's class and write something nice on their whiteboard. This quick little message might just be the boost they needed to turn their day around.

- Strategically place sticky notes with compliments on them throughout another teacher's daybook or textbooks. That way, every once and a while they will find one, and it will make their day.

- Make a staff room gift basket. Place it on the table with a quick note telling everyone that you enjoy working with them and learning from them. You do not need to be an administrator to do kind acts like this. It might mean even more to them, as it will be unexpected coming from you!

- Have students write one positive word to describe their teacher on a sticky note or piece of paper. Find a cool way to organize these words (i.e. create a Wordle online) and surprise the teacher with it.

- Create a fun game, like filling a container or cup with treats. Then, anonymously leave it on the desk of a co-worker with a note that encourages them to enjoy the treats and reciprocate by filling it and passing it on. This a great way to get everyone involved in spreading kindness throughout the staff.

- Blind lunch date. Send an anonymous letter inviting someone to join you for lunch. Set a time and location. When the time comes, bring in a lunch that you can both enjoy and explain to them that you wanted to do this because you enjoy spending time with them and you wanted to have a little fun!

When thinking of ways to be kind to staff, don't forget to include staff that might not receive as much attention as homeroom teachers do. Think of caretaking staff, crossing guards, lunchroom helpers, parent volunteers, administrative assistants, and anyone else who contributes to making school an amazing place.

KINDNESS TO YOURSELF

Often the hardest person to be kind to is yourself. Similar to the way we manage our self-care, we often tend to put ourselves last. We must give ourselves permission to be kind to us. Learning to build self-compassion and self-kindness into our lives is an important step in finding more happiness as an educator.

A great place to start is by thinking about how you are kind to other people. Make a list of ways that you show kindness, compassion, appreciation, recognition and respect to the people that you love. Take time to reflect on each act of kindness that you do for others, and ask yourself this question, "Do I treat myself the same way?"

Often, we do not. We tend to be tougher on ourselves. The message that we give those we care about, is often much different than the message we give ourselves. It is time to turn our kindness inwards. Here are ideas on how to do that:

Forgive Yourself

If your teaching partner bombed a lesson, you would not continually remind them about it all day. You would tell them that we all mess up and remind them about something awesome they did. We all make mistakes, and that is a good thing if we learn from them. Forgive yourself and try your best to make adjustments, that is all you can do. Getting over it starts with forgiveness.

Compliment Yourself

Part of being kind to others on staff is taking the time to comment on something great that you noticed about them. It could be a bulletin board, lesson idea, or even what they are wearing. Take some time each day to compliment yourself. By jotting these compliments down in a book or online, it will give you a place to turn when you are having a rough day and are feeling down on yourself.

Be Proud of Your Accomplishments

If a teacher on your staff was recognized for something great that they did and tried to downplay it completely, you would not accept that. You would tell them to be proud of it. You would remind them of all the hard work that they invested ,and you would want them to enjoy the praise. Try this one on yourself. When you work hard and are successful, enjoy and give yourself permission to be proud of yourself.

Pump Yourself Up

If one of your Teacher Friends Forever was down in the dumps, what would you do? You would try to pull them out of their slump. Perhaps you would try to make them laugh, motivate them or get them excited about something. So when you are feeling down, find ways to lift yourself back up. Perhaps it is blaring your favorite song on the drive to work, positive self talk, or a quick workout — do something that gets the positive vibes and energy flowing again.

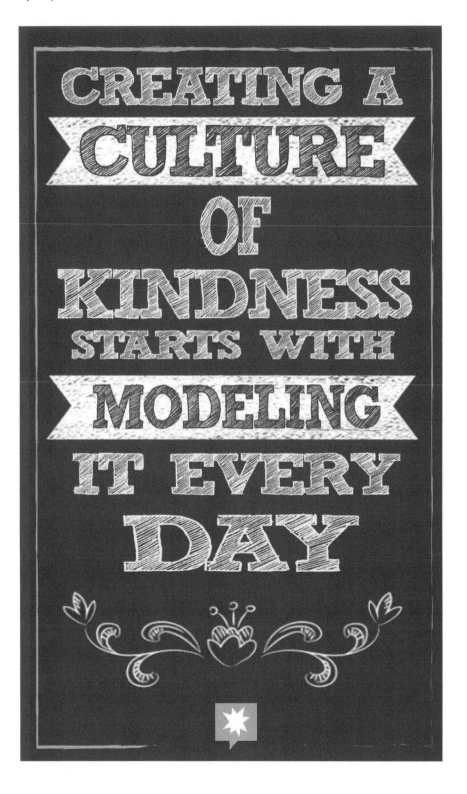

Give Yourself a Break

Part of being kind to someone is giving them a break when they need it so that they can refocus and readjust. It is easy to get overwhelmed as a teacher, especially at certain points in the school year. Recognize when you are running low on energy, patience, or focus. Know that giving yourself a short break is what you need to help you get through this busy or stressful time. This would be your advice to a friend. Give yourself the same advice.

Stand Up for Yourself

Part of being kind and being a good friend is standing up for someone that you care about. You would not let someone you love and respect fall under constant criticism and verbal abuse. You would stand up for them. Some of the worst criticism that we receive is from our own inner thoughts. Do not allow this negative self-talk to happen. Develop strategies that enable you to stand up to yourself and for yourself.

Care For Yourself

We talked about the importance of self-care earlier in this chapter. Consider each act of self-care you commit as an act of kindness to yourself. Do not look at these acts as being selfish or self-absorbed, look at them as a way to find more contentment in your life. By being kind to yourself, you will be in a better place to be kind to others.

Simple, Everyday Gestures

A lot of the ideas in this chapter are great ways to kickstart kindness in your school. They are different ways to get everyone thinking about being kind to others. However, remember kindness cannot just be a series of events at your school. We need to see kindness at something that we can build into every day through simple and meaningful gestures.

Never underestimate the power that holding a door open for someone or smiling and expressing gratitude can have on others. The best way to teach our students to perform these small, consistent acts of kindness is to model them daily to everyone around. They say that kindness is contagious — the more you practice it, the more it spreads.

Commit to doing acts of kindness in each of the following areas. Write your ideas in each of the boxes below.

KINDNESS IN THE CLASSROOM

KINDNESS IN THE SCHOOL

KINDNESS ON STAFF

KINDNESS TO YOURSELF

While completing each act of kindness, take time to reflect on the impact it has on your mood and the mood of others around you.

INNOVATE:
WHERE, WHO, WHAT
AND WHEN

*"You cannot discover new oceans unless you have the courage
to lose sight of the shore."*
— André Gide

One of my favorite methods of learning more about Happiness in
Education is running workshops. Often when I speak at a conference or at
professional learning days, I ask if I can run a workshop as well. By leading
educators through reflective activities, it gives me a great deal of insight
into the factors that have the most influence on their love of teaching.

To be honest, when I decided to start running workshops on Happiness
in Education, I had no idea what to expect. I did not know if people would
show up, and I was worried if they would be willing to share or engage in
discussions. Also, I was concerned that it could turn into a session about
why they were not happy in education. On all accounts, I was wrong.

As I watched teachers flow into the room for my first ever session,
I definitely had the first-day jitters. I was thankful that it was the session
right after lunch, and not the last session of the day. I could tell there was a
mix of curiosity and skepticism among the crowd. The session was designed
to be very interactive and to get the participants reflecting on how happy
they are in education.

The most telling activity of the session was the DOTmocracy. Around
the room, I posted 15 aspects of teaching that might bring joy to educators.

I gave each participant 36 red dots to place on the aspects of teaching that brought them the most happiness at the beginning of their career. Then I gave them 36 blue dots to place on the aspects of teaching that brought them the most happiness at this point in their career. This is where it got very interesting and intense.

As we were comparing the dot distribution on each aspect of teaching, we noticed that 'Planning Great Lessons' had dropped from 63 reds dots to 18 blue dots. So, I posed the question, "If planning great lessons is something that brought us a lot of happiness at the beginning of our careers, why does it no longer bring us that much happiness now?"

From the back of the room, I heard a loud groan of discontent. It startled me, and I played with the idea of ignoring it, but instead ,I probed a little deeper by asking the gentleman why he seemed so upset. His answer was amazing. He said, "For years, I have been walking around complaining that teaching is like groundhog day, and I just realized that I did it to myself."

He went on to explain that he had put a lot of red dots on 'planning great lessons' and zero blue dots. He talked about how that was his favorite part of teaching at the beginning of his career, and he was upset that somewhere along the line, he stopped investing in creating amazing lessons for his students.

Three weeks later, he tracked down my email to tell me that he decided to throw out all of the binders he had been teaching from and start from scratch. The last sentence in his email was, "Thank you, the happiness is back!"

My interaction with this teacher made me start to realize the importance that change and innovation have on teacher well-being. Over time, I began to notice that educators who are still motivated and happy in the latter part of their careers engage in continuous change and growth. This is what keeps them young, fulfilled, and energetic.

Innovate Your Career

To innovate means to make changes in something established, especially by introducing new methods or ideas.[120] It is about not settling for something that used to work. It is a willingness to seek out new learning experiences and take risks. As educators, it is not just teaching students how to become innovative lifelong learners, but living it ourselves.

I have been very fortunate to have conversations with many educators who recognize their willingness to change as one of the most important contributors to their love of education. Through these conversations, three key ideas that promote change and innovation emerged:

Listen to Your Life

We need to slow down and listen to what our life is telling us. For instance, if our life is telling us that 'Teaching is like Groundhog Day,' then we need to honor that and be willing to make the necessary changes to bring the happiness back. If our life is telling us that we are getting frustrated with the school and community we are teaching in, then we need to honor that and make a move. So often as educators, we rarely stop to think about ourselves and what we need. Listen to your life, and make the necessary changes to make it better.

Hold Ideas Lightly

I love this idea. Too often we get attached to an established way of doing things. We no longer do it because it is what we feel is best, we do it because it is what we have always done. We begin to get attached. With this attachment, eventually comes a resistance to change. For many of us, it is easier to hold on tightly to what we know than it is to try something new. This stifles our ability to change. Instead, we need to work on loosening our grip. We need to learn to let go of the way things were and look to find newer, cooler, better ideas.

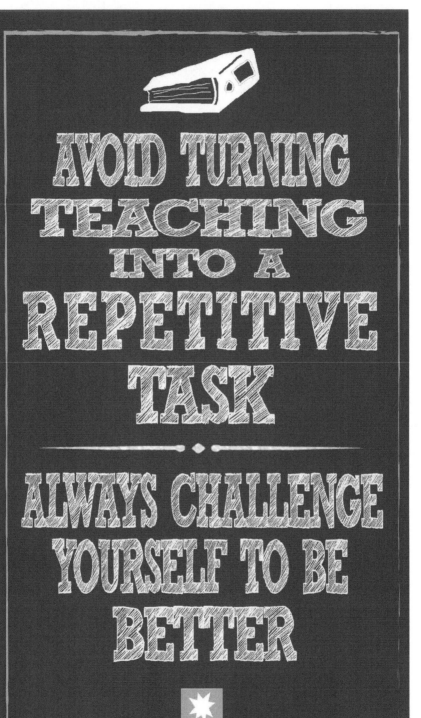

Admit Change is Necessary

Changing teacher practice is sometimes hard because essentially, we need to admit that what we had been doing in the past might not be as effective as what we are about to try. This is where we need to cut ourselves some slack. At that time, we were doing our best with what we had to work with. There is nothing to be ashamed of. We need to look at the old way of doing things as essentially building blocks to our new success. Be proud that you can recognize the need for change and that you are willing to try something new in hopes of getting better.

Keep Your Why, Change the Rest

Never lose focus on why you became an educator. We need to keep this at the forefront of everything that we do. This will be the driving force to keep us motivated, fulfilled, and happy. With our *why* locked in place, we need to be aware of *when* to make changes to *who*, *where* and *what* we teach.

Some of these changes will occur naturally over time, some will be made for you and for some you will need to step out of your comfort zone and take a risk. Learning to roll with the punches and embracing change as a chance for growth is a great mindset to develop.

This chapter will focus on some of the major career changes that can help reinvigorate educators. We are lucky to have so many options for change within the educational system and must make these changes when needed. The following chapter will focus on the importance of continuous change in HOW we teach. Both of these changes are necessary to thrive over the course of a teaching career.

Where We Teach

Often, we are the last ones to know when we need a change. It is not until it happens that we look back and realize that we really needed it. Occasionally in a workshop, I will encounter an educator who had been administratively transferred to another school. More often than not, they eventually reflect on this change in a positive way. They usually admit to being upset when it happened, but within a year they begin to see that it was time for them to move on.

For years, I tried to convince my sister that she needed to change schools. She had been teaching at the same school for 12 years. She was still doing amazing things and the community loved her; however you could feel that it was stunting her growth at times. On a whim, she finally decided to post out and move schools.

By changing her work environment and surrounding herself with new educators to learn from, she was happier than ever. I loved watching her push herself in new directions and develop new passions. We invited her to be a panel speaker at a leadership course that we run; she encouraged the audience to change schools often and to know that with each change comes a lot of unexpected, amazing things. I was so proud of her.

When I meet passionate educators, I love to ask them what their secret to maintaining their love of teaching is. On several occasions, I have heard the response, 'Self-Initiated 5-Year School Transfer'. For some educators, changing schools this often is a great way to promote continual growth. They embrace the challenge of supporting a new community and growing alongside a variety of different educators.

In saying that, I have met happy educators who have taught in the same building for a majority of their careers. They enjoy planting roots and developing deep relationships with the staff and community. These educators admit that it is essential for them to find ways to change and grow within the building.

It is often difficult to change schools. You are leaving the students you have grown to love, relationships you have established with staff, and the comfort of knowing what to expect. However, if you listen carefully to your life, you will know when it is time. Here are some common indicators that you might need a change:

- You are getting frustrated by seemingly small things that never frustrated you before. Changes within the way the building operates generate a negative emotional response.

- Getting motivated in the morning to go to work becomes more challenging. You feel like you are dragging yourself out the door and even the drive seems like a struggle.

- You are becoming more disconnected in staff meetings. You regularly feel like they are redundant, or the information seems irrelevant to you. Staying engaged is difficult.

- Everything that you hear going on at other schools sounds interesting and more fun. When you attend a district PD session, you become more curious about what other schools would be like to teach at.

- Your relationship with other educators or administration has deteriorated to the point that it is negatively impacting your desire to go to work. It seems unlikely that these issues will be resolved.

- Your stress level and physical health become more of an issue. You end up taking more time off as you feel work is a major source of your declining well-being.

Reflect honestly on your overall happiness at your school. Be willing to make the necessary changes if you find you are not where you need or want to be emotionally.

WHO WE TEACH

You love the building that you teach in. The staff, students, and community are exactly where you feel that you want to be. However, you start to feel that things are getting stale. There is a slow decline in the excitement you get delivering the curriculum to your class. You begin to get frustrated with your students quicker than you used to. Things that never used to bother you, now do. If this is the case, it might be time for a change in the grade or content area that you teach.

Each grade or content area can bring something new and refreshing to the table. For instance, students in the younger grades are blank canvases for the most part who are curious about learning and always entertaining. Middle grade students are keen to learn and are developing a sense of autonomy which can be very fulfilling to nurture. In the intermediate grades and beyond, you are able to have more mature conversations and relate to students on a different level. Often, we settle into our comfort zones with regard to the age of students that we teach, and this can limit our ability to continue to grow.

If contemplating a grade switch, write a pros and cons list for the grades or content that you might be interested in teaching. Take time to quickly explore the changes in the curriculum and the content that you are covering. If possible, sit in on different classes in your school or run an extracurricular activity focused on a different division. Taking the time to do a little research could lead you to teach a different grade or subject area that you end up really enjoying.

One of the keys is to be proactive about this type of change. Administrators are more likely to move you where you want if you approach them with your rationale. Try to let them know as soon as possible. That way, they can look for opportunities to help make the move happen. Depending on the size of the school, it can be difficult to move teachers internally without disrupting the entire staff. As soon as you know, let them know.

For some, changing grade level or subject matter might not even be enough. If you are looking for a whole new experience or audience, stepping out of the classroom and into a central role could be the change you need.

Becoming a resource teacher, consultant, coach, or administrator will feel like a career change. Although your job still focuses on students and learning, your day-to-day routines will be drastically different.

After 11 years of teaching the same grade, I decided it was time for a change. Over the years, I developed a passion for using technology in the classroom. So when a district-wide position supporting the use of technology was posted, I jumped on it. To be honest, I had many concerns about leaving the classroom. I knew I was going to miss the deep connections with my students and being part of a staff that spends a lot of time together.

I remember my first day in my new office space. I thought I had made the biggest mistake. The day was so uneventful and boring compared to the first day with a new class. Those first months took a lot of getting used to. However, by the midway point of the year, I started to really enjoy this position. What I loved most was getting to be in so many different classes and working with so many different educators. I saw it as a privilege to get this perspective on education.

In district-wide roles, you are constantly learning with and from other educators. This can be very fun and exciting. Whether you are delivering professional development in a workshop or co-teaching in a classroom, you are continually being challenged. As well, you get to take deep dives into the areas of the curriculum that you enjoy most. This can have a very positive impact on your level of happiness and your desire to come to work each day.

If I am being honest, I always think about going back to the classroom. I miss being with students throughout an entire school year. I miss that family feeling that develops within a classroom. However, I know that stepping away from this for a while will make me a happier and more impactful educator in the long run.

What We Teach

Sometimes all it takes to find a little more enjoyment in your teaching day is to teach something new or something that really interests you. You might not be interested in completely switching grades or schools; however, you feel the need for some change. Often these smaller changes require some maneuvering and/or creativity on your part.

Let your administrator know what your passions are and that you are interested in bringing them into your teaching. Be open with other teachers on staff about your desire to teach a specific subject. This could lead to a potential exchange of teaching assignments that could help both of you delve deeper into subjects of interest.

Understand that this can be difficult for administrators to support, especially in the beginning. It is always easier and safer to do things the way that they have always been done. Be patient, but also active in pursuing this change. The more you do outside of the classroom to demonstrate your passion and interest, the more likely your administration will be open to making this change.

For instance:
- Take an additional qualification course.
- Share your passion/knowledge at staff meetings.
- Attend Profession Development opportunities (i.e. workshops, conferences, etc.)
- Run extracurriculars relating to the subject.
- Make your passion visible throughout the school.
- Work toward being known as the 'Go-To' person in your school for that particular support.
- Volunteer your time in the community to deepen your understanding and to demonstrate your commitment.

Even if your administrators are unable to make the necessary arrangements to get you more teaching time in this area, it is still a worthwhile investment. It is always good to stay active in developing your signature skills. Eventually, there will come a time that you need a change. The more experience and knowledge you have in the areas of teaching that you love, the more likely it is you will get the position that you feel best suited for.

WHEN AND HOW MUCH CHANGE

The degree and amount of change that one needs is unique to each individual. It goes back to listening to your life. The better you can understand and anticipate your need for change, the more you will be prepared to make it.

Timing is an incredibly important factor when it comes to making major changes in teaching. There are going to be times in your life where too much change can cause an overload of stress. For instance, when my wife and I started our family, the thought of changing anything other than diapers caused panic attacks. Luckily, I had been teaching the same grade for several years and had a solid base that helped me survive this busy time.

IT WILL PROBABLY NEVER FEEL LIKE THE **PERFECT TIME** TO PURSUE A MAJOR CHANGE

SOMETIMES YOU JUST NEED TO TAKE **THE RISK**

Understand that it will never seem like the perfect time to make a major change. Teaching is always busy, and you constantly feel like there is so much more you can do. However, there are periods of time throughout our careers where change is possible. Try not to get stuck into believing that you are too busy to change if needed.

Be honest with yourself and accept that change can be difficult and a lot of work, but in the long run, it will have a positive impact on how much you love your job.

Listen to your life carefully and rate on the scales below your level of happiness in each of the categories listed. Let one represent that you need a change desperately, ten represent you absolutely love it.

COMMUNITY

1   2   3   4   5   6   7   8   9   10

SCHOOL

1   2   3   4   5   6   7   8   9   10

GRADE

1   2   3   4   5   6   7   8   9   10

SUBJECTS

1   2   3   4   5   6   7   8   9   10

STAFF

1   2   3   4   5   6   7   8   9   10

REFLECTION QUESTIONS

Analyze these numbers carefully. Anything under a 7 tells you that you should start thinking of a possible change in the aspect of your job. What categories fall in this range? Are there small changes you can make with regard to this category?

Anything under 5 tells you that you need a change. Weigh your options and do not be afraid of that risk. You deserve to love what you do everyday. What major change could you make to improve this rating?

Repeat this exercise each year to ensure that you are listening to your life and making changes when needed.

INNOVATE:
How We Teach

"If we teach today as we taught yesterday,
we rob our children of tomorrow."
— John Dewey

My friend invited me to attend an event in which Tony Robbins was speaking. I had not seen this friend in a while, so I accepted. When we arrived, I could not believe the number of people there. I would estimate there were over 20,000 attendees. Without a doubt, this was the most intense talk I had ever seen. For over three hours, he had us dancing, crying, cheering, and thinking. It was incredibly powerful.

My biggest take away from hearing him speak was his message around 'Progress equals happiness.' As an educator, this made so much sense. It helped me realize what I loved most about being a teacher. I loved watching students make progress from the beginning of the year until the end. I found it very satisfying to see them grow academically, socially, and/ or emotionally. It was their progress that brought me joy.

I also started to understand the importance of personal growth within this profession. As I reflected on my career, I could see that the happiest times were ones in which I was working hard to achieve something. Conversely, during the times that I encountered the most amount of struggle, I was resistant to change and making limited progress.

At this time, I was working with hundreds of educators each month. I became fascinated with the correlation between a teacher's happiness and their desire to continually grow as educators. Regardless of what way I looked at it, Tony Robbins was right. Progress does equal happiness.

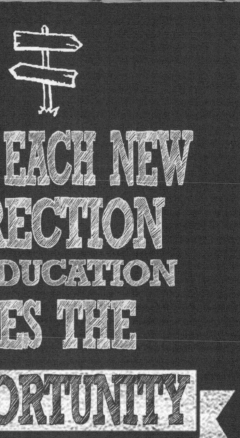

Authentic Annual Learning Plan

For some educators, continually changing how to teach comes naturally. They are intrinsically motivated to learn and change throughout their careers. They hold ideas lightly and are open to experimenting with new approaches to teaching.

However, for educators like myself, change is not as easy. We need to methodically build growth into each year. By developing a plan, we can greatly increase the likelihood that we will continue to grow within the profession.

Many districts will ask educators to complete an Annual Learning Plan (ALP) each year. It is good in theory; however, often, it can lack authenticity. Because these are usually tied into our evaluations, it is hard to be honest. We end up committing to professional development our administrators feel strongly about and that tie into our school goals. I still think this has value as far as the school is concerned, however, I would argue the personal learning needs are not always met.

If you are someone who struggles to make changes to your teaching style, it might be a good idea to develop your own Authentic Annual Learning Plan. Before the school year starts, reflect on areas of your teaching that you would like to make changes to. Write these changes down, then prioritize which ones you will work on throughout the year. You cannot work on everything at once, so pick a couple of goals that excite you and that you look forward to working on.

Done correctly, creating a plan will actually reduce the amount of stress you experience with regard to professional development. Unchanneled motivation can be destructive as it can leave you feeling overwhelmed and unfulfilled. If you spend the entire year trying to be great at every aspect of teaching, you will either burn out or not be satisfied with the results. Increase the likelihood of success by keeping your learning at a manageable level.

Personally, I like to try to get really good at one thing every year. I make it my own personal mission to push my own learning and add one valuable teaching skill to my repertoire. Taking a deep dive into personal learning can be very fulfilling and motivating.

Be Grateful for the Pendulum Swing

In my first year of teaching, I had a conversation with a more experienced teacher after a staff meeting. She explained to me that it was not worth investing in what we were learning as a staff, as the focus was going to change as soon as we finally got it. She mentioned that this is a pattern that she has seen many times throughout her career.

As I reflect on this 15 years later, she was partially right. The pedagogical focus has changed several times since then. However, where she was wrong was her perspective on the value of these changes.

Later that year, I discussed this with another teacher on staff who truly loved her job. She shared with me her perspective on how changes in district focus has had a very positive impact on her career. This teacher chooses to see each pendulum swing as a nudge to help her change and grow as an educator. She went on to say that with each change in direction brings new teaching strategies and new ways to help students learn.

I recall asking her if she is ever frustrated, knowing that all of the effort she invested in a particular method of teaching is no longer a focus. Her reply was amazing. She explained that when there is a change or shift in focus, she leaves behind what was not working for her and only brings with her the learning that was valuable. It reminded me of decluttering my home. I keep everything that has value and throw out the rest.

However, it is important to realize that just because I no longer needed something, does not mean it did not have value at some point.

It all comes down to perspective and how you choose to see the world. Happy educators do not see change as merely more work, they see it as an opportunity to grow and be better for their students. Work on developing an appreciation for learning and professional development within education. For some educators, this will eventually be the difference between loving their jobs or not.

Nothing Better To Do

As a grade eight teacher, it never fails to amaze me the scope of engagement in every class I taught. Despite all being a part of the same lessons, each student's experience was much different from the next. Some students hung on every word and laughed at every bad joke. Whereas other students rolled their eyes and were bored to death. Each student's experience was highly influenced by their perception of learning and school.

Each year, I would make it one of my primary goals to shift those who were disengaged over to the engaged side. One of my go to moves was my 'Nothing Better to do' lecture. Here is the Coles Notes version of this conversation:

Me: How many hours a day do you attend classes?
Student: I don't know?

Me: Let me help you. You are in class five hours a day; that is 30 hours/week and almost 1000 hours/year. That is a lot of time!

Student: You are telling me.

Me: When you are sitting in class, what are your options of things to do?

Student: What do you mean?

Me: You either engage or do nothing. You can either spend 1000 hours bettering yourself, or sit there bored. There are no other options. You have nothing better to do during this time because you are stuck in a classroom with me. Right?

Student: Yup.

Me: Watch the other students who make the decision to learn, they are happier and are even having fun at times. They are getting something out of this. It is not as painful for them. I challenge you to try it for a while. I bet it is better than sitting there bored out of your mind all day.

Student: I guess?

I imagine that I am not the first teacher to give this lecture, and I won't be the last. That is because as educators we want our students to invest in themselves. We understand that the more they invest, the more they will enjoy coming to school each day. This same logic applies to educators. The more we invest in our learning, the happier we'll be coming to work each day.

I give myself this lecture when I am in a staff meeting or workshop. My two options are to disengage and be bored, or I can engage and maybe learn something. I have already committed my time to be there, so I might as well make it meaningful.

Just as some students find it hard to stay focused and engaged during long bouts of learning, so do educators. Here are a few tips on how to get the most out of professional development.

TAKE NOTES

To help stay focused and increase learning, take notes while listening. The research shows that "we tend to lose almost 40% of new learning within 24 hours of first reading or hearing it".[121] By taking notes, you are more likely to positively benefit from the learning that is being presented. If you want to take notetaking to the next level, try sketchnoting. This is a fun way to organize your notes in a visual way that is meaningful to you.

Participate

Making it a goal to participate in discussions during professional learning is a great way to ensure that you are staying focused. Try to ask questions, share ideas and voice opinions. Not only will this keep you more connected to the conversation, it will also help deepen your understanding of the content. Avoid dominating the conversation or talking to talk. Look for key opportunities to add value. Also, never ask a question just as the staff meeting is about to end. This is how you lose teacher friends!

Remove Distractions

If you really want to increase the likelihood of learning more during professional development, avoid unnecessary distractions such as your device or computer (unless of course it is a technology-based session). It is so easy to slip into organizing your Google Drive or scrolling through pictures. Simple rule — if it takes away from your learning, then you are better off without it.

Don't Just Wait for PD

I have been fortunate to attend many conferences throughout my career. In my opinion, this is one of the most inspiring atmospheres in education. The educators who attend are always extremely excited, positive, collaborative and happy. They are looking to learn and connect with other educators who want to learn as well.

My personal opinion is that all educators should have the opportunity to experience this. Too often, we see professional development as something that is provided for us and not something that we seek out. We need to take some control over our own learning and find ways to immerse ourselves in professional development that works for us.

If attending a conference is not in the budget, you can experience similar types of learning by developing a Personal Learning Network online or with other teachers in your district. I love when I hear that a group of teachers are connecting to learn and plan outside of mandated district PD. They get to decide what the learning looks like, and they can contour it so that it works for them. From my experience, the teachers who take part in this type of learning are always among the happiest around.

Using the Curriculum To Grow

"Where do I start?" This is one of the most common questions teachers ask themselves when they are asked to teach a new grade or subject.

Curriculum documents serve as a guide for teachers and ensure that student learning is sequential and well-rounded. Beyond that, the curriculum can be used as a tool to advance teacher growth and engagement throughout their careers.

The further we advance into our career, the more important it is to regularly revisit these documents. Just because the curriculum expectations have not changed, does not mean that the manner in which we interpret and approach them has to be the same. New learning will enable us to make changes to our program that will excite us and improve student learning.

My appreciation for the power of curriculum started when I worked alongside an incredible teacher. At that time, I was creating fun projects that students could delve into and enjoy from start to finish. Those assignments were linked directly to the curriculum expectations, however, after working alongside this teacher I soon realized that these lessons could have more substance to deepen student learning.

It took a while for me to realize that her approach was more effective in many ways than what I had been doing. I began to understand and watched her artistry as she taught the curriculum. It used to frustrate me at the beginning when we started planning. My first instinct was to think of something fun, whereas her first instinct was to analyze her student needs and the curriculum to find natural ties that would develop the necessary skills. Over time, I developed more of an understanding and began to see positive results in student learning and performance. Knowing my students were learning better became a motivating factor for change.

By learning to use the curriculum more effectively, I began to develop great pride and enjoyment in planning new units and concepts. My planning was no longer just part of the job, it was a challenge. This helped increase the engagement of both myself and my students. They were energized by these lessons that honed their skills, while exploring content that we were all passionate about.

There is so much more to the curriculum than simply going through it like a checklist. That can quickly become boring for both you and your students. Look at the finer details and natural connections within it. For instance, my former teaching partner always focused on the verbs used in each expectation. It matters whether it said, 'identify' or 'investigate.' The word investigate led to deeper learning experiences than the word identify. These small changes in wording would drive her planning in an entirely different direction and the result was always a better learning experience.

At no point does teaching curriculum need to be boring. It is imperative to not just develop students academically, but to also make

meaningful connections to and for them. Learning to do this takes time, experience, and effort. As we become better at it, our love for teaching will continually grow.

USING STUDENTS TO GROW

Our greatest ally to ensure we change throughout our careers is our students. Each new class brings a wealth of skills, knowledge ,and passions that we can tap into to help us evolve how we teach. No longer is the teacher the only one who holds and dispenses the knowledge.

Technology has put learning in the hands of our students, and they are using it. In a study of the Generation Z group, 59% preferred Youtube as a learning preference.[122] Our students now have the ability to deepen their own learning on any topic they choose whenever they like. Some educators might see this as a shift in power, whereas others will see it as an opportunity to push their own learning.

Countless times in my role as technology consultant I have met students that blow my mind regarding their understanding of coding. When I ask them how they know so much, they usually respond, 'Youtube'. I find it incredible how much they can learn on their own when they find something they love. Not only that, I am usually impressed with their ability to pass on this knowledge to myself or other students in the class.

Embracing this change in education is paramount. Educators who are open to learning from their students tend to enjoy coming to work more. It makes each day more exciting knowing that you are not just going to teach the lesson, but also learning during the lesson. To create this environment in the classroom, we must promote more student agency by helping our students learn through meaningful, relevant activities that are self-initiated and driven by their interests.

Here are some suggestions on how to support a classroom that is alive and overflowing with passion:

TEACH MORE SKILLS AND LESS CONTENT

Allow students to find and curate more of the content they need, while you teach them how to collaborate, research, organize and plan more effectively.

COMMIT TO A NEW LEARNING CULTURE

To do this effectively, it needs to be a part of the culture, not just an event that occurs once and a while. From day one, promote a culture of learning together and express an interest in their knowledge.

Don't Save Them Right Away

Too often, we jump in too fast. Allow them to struggle — that is the most important part of the learning. It is more important to teach them how to approach issues and tackle them than it is to help them solve it.

Teach Scaffolding

As educators, we are good at breaking down learning into manageable chunks for our students. Teach them this skill, do not do it for them. This is a valuable skill they need to learn. Just scaffold them on how to scaffold.

Fan Their Passions

When a student is excited about something, join in that excitement with them. Show interest by asking questions and assuming the learner role. Empower them to be the teacher during this conversation.

Help Them Give Effective Feedback

Feedback is essential to student success. To promote student agency, encourage 'student-to-self' feedback. You won't always be there, so help them learn the importance of self-reflection and teach them how to do this more effectively.

Enjoy their Journey

Learn to let go and take time to enjoy all of the learning in the room. Try to learn something new from each student. In my experience, learning from students who are happy is always much better than teaching students who are bored.

From a happiness perspective, we should be grateful for the shift from the old way of teaching to the new. By increasing the students' access to content, it allows us to create a job that is ever changing and fun. We no longer need to deliver lesson after lesson at the front of the classroom. Although there might be comfort in this at the beginning, over time it becomes automatic and emotionless. Bring the fun and excitement back into teaching by redefining your role in their learning.

Changing how we teach throughout our careers is challenging. It takes a lot of time and commitment. We must realize that we will never achieve mastery in this profession. However, we should never stop trying.

In his book, *Drive*, Daniel Pink says that 'Mastery is an Asymptote.'[123] He explains that no matter how good you get at something, there is always room for improvement. We must always remember that the joy lies in the pursuit and that we should always strive to be better. That is what makes coming to work interesting and fun. It is also what will keep us relevant and effective in the classroom.

1. Putting district and school goals aside, which areas of teaching would you love to explore? In the box provided, brainstorm different personal professional development goals that you have.

2. Highlight one goal from this list that you feel you would enjoy learning about the most and would love to implement into your teaching repertoire.

3. Commit right now to making this your goal for the next year.

4. In the box below, brainstorm the different resources, contacts and avenues to begin this journey. Remember that this journey is for your enjoyment. Do not rush yourself or pressure yourself so much that it stresses you out. Approach this with consistency, not intensity, and enjoy the journey.

VIABILITY:
Peaks and Valleys

"Between peaks there are always valleys.
How you manage your valley determines
how soon you reach your next peak."
— *Spencer Johnson*

Viability is defined as the ability to survive or live successfully, especially under certain conditions.[124] It involves being able to adapt and persevere to make it through the tough times. As educators, there will be tough times, and there will be struggles. Just as there will be many amazing moments and triumphs. We need to learn to embrace both fully if we want to have truly amazing careers.

One of my favorite authors is Spencer Johnson. He is a creative genius when it comes to telling fables that teach us valuable life lessons. In his book, Peaks and Valleys, he takes us on the journey of a young man who is dissatisfied in his life. Eventually, the main character decides to make the trek from the valley he lives in to one of the peaks above. When he arrives, he meets a wiseman who offered to share with him the Peaks and Valleys Philosophy of Living a Better Life. The young man accepts the offer and here is some of the knowledge the wiseman shares:[125]

- Everyone experiences peaks and valleys.
- To obtain more peaks, we must learn to manage valleys.
- What we do in bad times shapes the good times.
- To change a valley into a peak, we must either change the situation itself or how we feel about this situation.

- To find our way out of a valley, we must choose to see things differently, learn from the situation and use that knowledge to improve the situation.

These lessons, and many others given throughout the book strongly support the conversations I have with educators who maintain a love of teaching throughout their careers. They admit to having tougher years and being in valleys, but share with pride how they reconnected with their passion to teach.

We All Experience Peaks and Valleys

One of my favorite activities to do with groups of educators is to have them create a Happiness Timeline on a graph that represents their teaching career (see Happiness Homework in Part One of this book). In all of the times that I have done this with educators, not once has anyone drawn a straight line or one that gradually goes up or down.

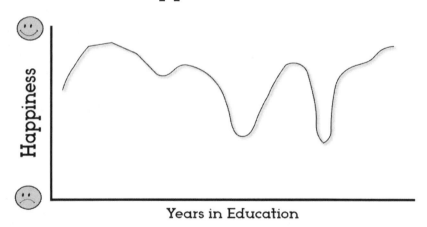

Often their graph looks similar to my graph. There is a series of highs and lows, that represent the peaks and valleys of their careers. It is interesting to listen to each person share the stories behind their timeline. They often light up when they talk about their best years, and generally look frustrated when sharing their tough years. However, when you ask them about how they were able to climb out of a valley, they usually explain a valuable lesson that they learned from being in it.

In my opinion, there is nothing sadder in education than a teacher who lands in a valley and never gets out. Going to work becomes a struggle and a place of resentment. They become jaded and frustrated with the system and no longer find happiness or fulfillment in this career. It is sad, but it does not need to be this way.

Explanatory Style

Charles Swindoll once said, "life is 10% what happens to me and 90% of how I react to it." [126] I believe this to be true in education. When I reflect on the two major valleys in my career, I can now admit that it had less to do with what happened to me, and everything to do with how I chose to handle it.

As I look back on what initiated these tough times in my career, I realized that there were others around me who experienced the same conditions. However, they chose not to let it affect them as deeply as I let it affect me. They worked hard and made decisions that allowed them to still find enjoyment in their jobs. Their valleys were shallow and shorter in duration, compared to mine that seemed daunting.

It goes back to the realities that we create, what we choose to focus on, and what we choose to let go of. In Martin Seligman's book Learned Optimism, he presents the idea that positivity can be learned like a skill through changing our self-talk. He says that it is possible to make the shift from pessimism to optimism. [127]

Seligman breaks down how we process the world around us into what he calls Explanatory Styles. A pessimist's explanation of what is happening is much different than an optimist. He says it comes down to the three P's; Personalization, Permanence, and Pervasiveness. [128]

Personalization is deciding who is at fault. Pessimists believe that they are usually to blame. Optimists, on the other hand, are less likely to assume full responsibility.

Permanence refers to how long you feel that an event is going to cause you suffering. Optimists tend to view negative events as temporary. They know they will pass over time. Whereas, pessimists struggle to see the situation ever being resolved.

Pervasiveness is the belief that a negative situation is going to affect all areas of your life. Optimists are better at compartmentalizing negatives, whereas pessimists allow negatives in one area of their lives to transfer to others.

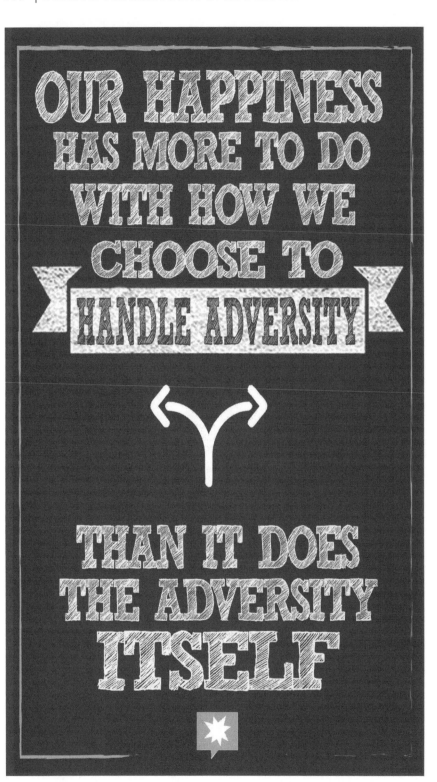

Here is an example of how an optimist and a pessimist might view a situation at a school differently. Let's say that you have a parent that has expressed an issue with the way a situation was handled at school. How might you explain this situation in your mind?

A more pessimistic person would often blame themselves, feeling that they could have prevented it if they would have acted sooner or made a different decision (personalization). They might then feel that this parent will never trust them again and that they have ruined the relationship (permanence). Following that, they might think that this issue will spill into the community and affect other relationships taking away from their credibility in the profession (pervasiveness).

A more optimistic person would have a different view of their role in the situation. They might take credit for their part in the problem, but they would not accept blame if it was not warranted (personalization). They would feel that this situation would probably blow over, as did others of similar magnitude in the past (permanence). Finally, they would be less likely to feel that this situation would impact their credibility beyond this one parent (pervasiveness).

It is worth mentioning that you are neither one nor the other. View this as a continuum in which you can move from one side to the other. Seligman stresses that there are times where taking a more pessimistic approach has its advantages. For instance, if a decision involves a lot of risk, it is good to be a little skeptical. Likewise, if you are too optimistic, you might not take responsibility or precautions that are needed to make the right decision.[129]

Just being more aware of your inner thoughts is a great first step towards becoming more optimistic. Take time to reflect on your explanatory style and how it impacts your mood, how you view situations and how you react. Don't be afraid to challenge your negative thoughts and prove them wrong. Try to be patient with this process and understand that it takes time to rewire your brain; however, believe that it is possible and worth trying for.

Believing You Can Make the Climb

Permanence can prolong our stay in the valleys. If we are unable to see a positive outcome, it makes it difficult to start the climb. Initiating forward progress is the challenging part when times are tough. It requires us to take a deep breath, control our thinking, and view the situation through other lenses. We must start to believe that things can get better before we take the first step.

Through my struggles in education, I have employed several strategies that help motivate me to get out of my valleys quicker. They are:

- Make a list of other struggles that I have faced and overcome. I use this list to convince myself that I can do it again.

- Look for examples of people who have overcome hardship to find happiness. Whether it be my friends, other teachers, or even people online, I find seeing others overcome life's hurdles motivating.

- Share my struggles with my TFFs or PLN. By asking others in the profession for their honest insights and suggestions, I feel that they might help me see the situation through a more positive lens.

- Write out different realities of the situation I am struggling with. I try to be as subjective as possible. Often this helps me realize that the valley is not as deep as I think.

- Continue to practice gratitude and other habits that positively shape the way I see the world. I have discovered that this is the time that I need these routines in my life the most.

It is all about getting the ball rolling in the right direction. Sometimes tackling the major issue that you are dealing with is overwhelming. If that is the case, look to find more joy in ways that have worked for you in the past. Perhaps you commit to doing acts of kindness for others or focus on reestablishing self-care habits that make you feel better. Allow yourself to reconnect to that feeling of joy that you have been missing and build from there.

When working your way out of a valley, expect setbacks. Challenge yourself to view them differently. Work on seeing struggle as an opportunity for growth. Reflect on struggles that you have overcome and dig deeply to find the lessons that you have learned. With each setback and struggle you overcome, you build momentum and confidence. Celebrate and savor the process of finding more contentment. Find joy in knowing that you have more control than you have given yourself credit for in the past.

PRACTICE HAPPINESS AT ALL ALTITUDES

Enjoying life and education is too important to leave up to chance. Whether we are in a valley or on a peak, we must invest in routines and habits that make us happier. However, from my experience, it is easier to develop healthier habits when times are good. It is similar to preventative healthcare. Instead of waiting until we are sick to treat the issue, we can take measures that will prevent us from illness.

For instance, practicing gratitude using the *Happyfeed* app has been one of the most impactful additions to my happiness routines. I discovered this app midway through writing this book, and I was in a really great place in both my work and personal life. *Happyfeed* quickly became something that I looked forward to every night. I loved that it helped me highlight all of the great aspects of each day.

Unfortunately, later that year, my mom ended up in the hospital, and we received devastating news regarding her health. We spent many days and nights with her at the hospital. It was a really tough time for all of us. However, each night when I got home, I would get a notification on my phone, reminding me to upload three moments of gratitude. As tough as this was, it really helped me pull out positives from the day.

By having a gratitude routine in place, it aided me through this really tough period in my life. It would have been very easy to slip into a bad place that would have been difficult to recover from. Had I waited until times were tough, I am not sure if I would have been willing or able to integrate this routine into my life. Throughout this trying time, I did not miss one entry of gratitude, and I still use it every day.

SUMMER REBOOT

Many educators are fortunate enough to get a well-deserved extended break from teaching over the summer. This profession can be exhausting and can really wear you down throughout the year. We invest so much emotion into our students, it can be hard to invest it into ourselves. It is vital that we learn to use our summers as a time of both reflection and rejuvenation.

Usually, I like to take the first week off to decompress. I find that my brain is still in teaching mode and slows down gradually throughout this week. By the second week, I am thinking clearly again. I find that this is the best time for me to reflect on my year. I like to think back to the highs and the lows; figure out what I did well and what I need to work on. It is also a great opportunity to reflect on where we are at with regard to our overall happiness in the profession. I find quantifying it helps. Give yourself a happiness in education rating between 1 and 10. One being very unhappy, ten being extremely happy.

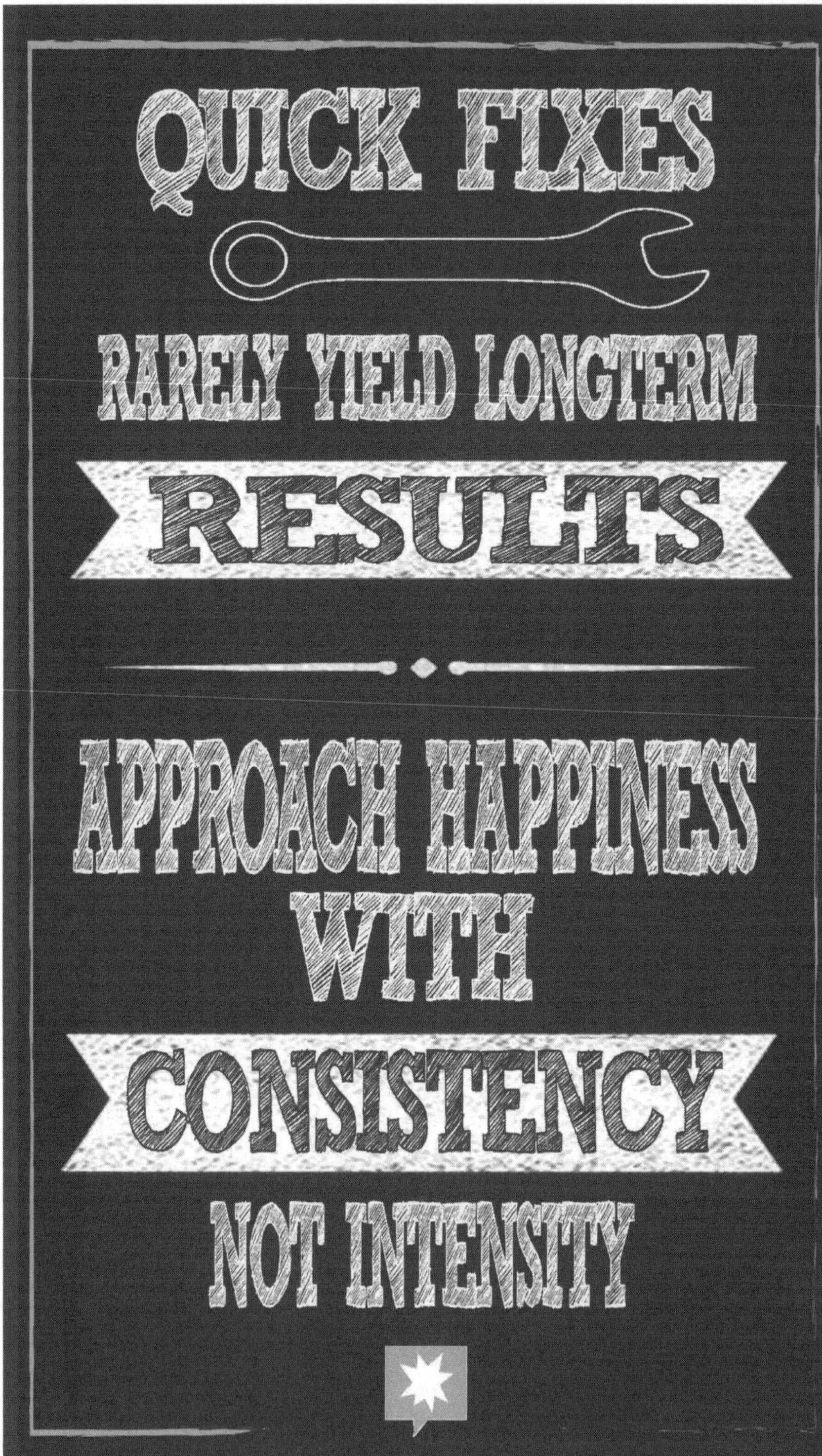
QUICK FIXES
RARELY YIELD LONGTERM
RESULTS
APPROACH HAPPINESS
WITH
CONSISTENCY
NOT INTENSITY

If your number is six or lower, this tells you that you are in a valley. This is an indicator that you need to make some changes that will bring more enjoyment into your school life. Brainstorm and make a list of what it is that is bringing this number down. From that list, highlight the aspects that you have control over. Avoid getting caught up thinking about things that you do not have the ability to change. Invest your energy in determining what personal changes you need to make to bring more happiness into the following year.

If your number is seven or above, ask yourself what it is you are doing that is bringing you so much joy. As the answers come to you, commit to investing in these areas again the following year. Whether it is learning or relationships, value the impact it is having on your teaching career. Also, take the time to savor that you are on or near a peak. Do not take it for granted-make a point of enjoying it and remembering it.

Summer is a great time to invest in all of those things that we wanted to do throughout the year, but were too busy. This is our opportunity to devote more time to self-care, our passions, and the people that we love. Not many professions give you the opportunity each year to reset and establish new routines that will contribute to your overall well-being. Make the most of it. This is an amazing perk of the job.

INTENSITY VERSUS CONSISTENCY

Often when we try to make changes in our lives, we attack them with intensity. We go all in at an unrealistic level that is difficult or impossible to maintain. Life eventually interferes with our lofty expectations, and we give up. Or we try something new and expect a quick fix. We are often disappointed when it does not yield the result that we had hoped for. This becomes discouraging and we give up.

From my experience, building more happiness into our lives has more to do with consistency than it does intensity. It is a slower process, one that requires us to make small changes that we build into our way of living. We must trust that if we invest in ourselves and what makes us happy, we will eventually arrive where we want to be. They key is that we do not stop striving to be happier.

Too often, we try to build a new habit into our lives, and we give up before it has time to show its true impact. I experienced this with practicing mindfulness. After reading a couple of really convincing books on this subject, I decided to jump right in. Right off the bat, I wanted to learn how to meditate. I watched videos, downloaded apps, and read everything that I could about it.

Each day I would sit cross-legged in the traditional position that I had seen many times before. I worked intensely at trying to slow down my thoughts and get into the zone. Within minutes, my back was sore, my right foot was asleep, and I was feeling anything but calm and mindful. Of all the routines I tried to implement while writing this book, this was one that frustrated me the most. I found this very ironic.

Eventually, I gave up. My explanation to myself was that mindfulness was something that just was not meant for me. Over a year later, I attended a positive education conference and one of the keynote speakers, David Mochel (www.appliedattention.com), was presenting on mindfulness.[130] He started off his talk getting the audience into a comfortable position and focused on their breathing. As we were doing this, every so often, he would gently say, "If your mind has wandered, just bring it back." With 100% accuracy, every time he said this, my mind was somewhere else.

This confirmed to me that mindfulness was just not for me. That was until he asked the whole audience, "Whose mind was wandering the majority of times I said that?" Pretty much the entire audience raised their hands, and everyone started to laugh. I felt strangely validated, knowing everyone was struggling with this too. In a very convincing and humorous manner, he went on to explain that the process of bringing your attention back to your breath is an exercise in mindfulness.

This was a huge 'aha' moment for me. I realized that my failed attempts at practicing mindfulness were due to the intensity that I approached it. Trying to jump right into deep meditation and expecting enlightenment was beyond unrealistic and set me up for failure.

Now, thanks to David, I realize that becoming more mindful is a process that takes time and consistency to develop. We need to find ways to build it into our everyday lives so that it becomes part of who we are and what we do daily. At this point, I am still just working on connecting to my breathing and developing more awareness of the sensations occurring throughout my body. These exercises do not take a lot of time, and I find myself really enjoying becoming more mindful.

Sometimes to get out of valleys, we need to take this approach. We need to trust that the habits and routines that have been shown to positively affect happiness and well-being will work if we stick to them long enough. We need to approach them in a way that will work for us and that we know we can maintain and build on.

One Step at a Time

Martin Luther King Jr. said, "You don't have to see the whole staircase, just take the first step."[131] Getting out of a valley can seem intimidating if you focus on how far you are from the peak. That is why it is usually best to just focus on what is right in front of you and what you can control. Just believe that you are worth it and that you will make it there if you just keep moving in the right direction.

Look back to the Happiness Timeline you completed in Part One of this book (pg. 17). Select the deepest valleys in your career so far and use these valleys to answer the questions below.

1. Summarize in two sentences why you felt this was the toughest period of your career.

    _____

    _____

    _____

    _____

2. Reflect on this period now- what decisions did you make that made this situation worse?

3. Did you approach this period in your career with optimism or pessimism? Use Martin Seligman's 3P (Personalization, Permanence and Pervasiveness) to help you analyze the situation.

    _____

4. How could you have found your way out of the valley quicker?

    _____

    _____

    _____

VIABILITY:
NAVIGATING THROUGH STRESS

"The greatest weapon against stress is our
ability to choose one thought over another."
— William James

Simply put, teaching is hard. It is a high-stress, high-stakes profession that can easily wear you down. Teacher burnout is on the rise, and more teachers are choosing to leave the profession than ever before. For instance, in Canada, the United States and the United Kingdom, approximately 40% of new teachers will leave the profession in their first 5 years.[132]

It is not just new teachers who are feeling this way. Research also shows that 46% of teachers report "high daily stress, which compromises their health, sleep, quality of life, and teaching performance."[133] Learning to navigate and manage stress as an educator is one of the most critical aspects of maintaining our love of teaching.

As someone who has the opportunity to work with thousands of educators each year, I can see the impact that stress is having on the profession. Although these stats are scary, I like to focus on the fact that many educators are able to successfully cope with this stress and find true happiness in teaching. It reminds me that it is possible if I am willing to maintain a positive focus and healthy work-life balance.

COMPASSION OVERLOAD

As class sizes and student needs grow, so does the demand on the teacher. This goes well beyond an increase in planning and marking. There is an emotional component which is required to meet the needs of every student.

To help them succeed, we must be willing to open our hearts and let them in. This can be very fulfilling, but at the same time emotionally exhausting.

The greater the needs and struggles within a class, the greater the stress on the educator. Helping students to work through trauma can be especially wearing on a teacher's emotions. It is very difficult to detach and leave this stress at work. It is easy to allow the struggles our students are facing to take over our lives.

Teaching, like nursing and social work, is considered a caring profession. We are responsible for the well-being of those in our care. This puts us at risk for what is known as compassion fatigue. It is a form of burnout characterized by extreme mental, emotional, and spiritual exhaustion.[134] We are at high risk for this if our students are suffering through traumatic experiences. We need to be aware of the impact this can have on our well-being and we must have strategies in place to help us manage this stress.

ASK FOR HELP

Often when we are overwhelmed with needs in our class, we tend to put our heads down and struggle through it alone. We must voice our need for extra support and resources. Often these students will need experts in different areas to get the full support that they need. It is not a weakness to ask for help.

DON'T BE HARD ON YOURSELF

Do the best you can to support these students, but know that sometimes no matter what you do, you might not be able to help them. Come to terms with the fact that there are many factors outside of your control at play. Be proud of the effort and care you have provided each student, and try not to internalize it too much.

LET SOMEONE TAKE CARE OF YOU

During those tough times where you are feeling emotionally drained, find support for yourself. Whether that be colleagues, friends, loved ones or professionals, surround yourself with people you can confide in and who support your needs. Take care of yourself, so you can take care of your students better.

PRIZED POSSESSIONS

In my experience, the only thing tougher than dealing with a difficult student is dealing with a difficult parent/guardian. They can be the source of an amazing amount of stress for educators if they are not happy. Learning how to gain and maintain the trust of a parent community can have an extremely positive effect on your experience at a school.

Always remember that parents truly love their children and want what is best for them. When they are upset, it is because they are trying to protect and support someone they care for deeply. They entrust us with their prized possessions each day and have high expectations that their needs will be met.

That is why effective parent communication is one of the best investments an educator can make. Not only does it help to keep parents/guardians in the loop of what is going on, it also builds confidence and reduces anxiety. Getting parents on board means you will spend less time in the long run dealing with issues. This will reduce stress and allow you to enjoy teaching more.

Not only that, the relationships we culture with parents can turn out to be positive in many ways. Happy parents are usually very supportive and willing to help when needed. I am always amazed how generous they can be with their time and resources if they respect the work you are doing for their child. As well, these parents help to keep you updated on the students when they are no longer in your care. I love meeting parents in the community and hearing all of the adventures that my former students are experiencing.

When trying to establish these positive relationships with parents, keep some of the following suggestions in mind:

Make contact right away

The first week of school can produce a lot of anxiety for parents and students. Make an effort to connect with each parent to introduce yourself. These short conversations let the parents know that you are invested in and excited to teach their children.

Commit to consistent communication

Finding an efficient way to keep parents in the loop can really help build their confidence. Whether you are using a website, app or paper communication, commit to a schedule and stick to it. Too often, we start off strong and then fade as the year goes on. Make sure that you are able to maintain the same level of communication throughout the year.

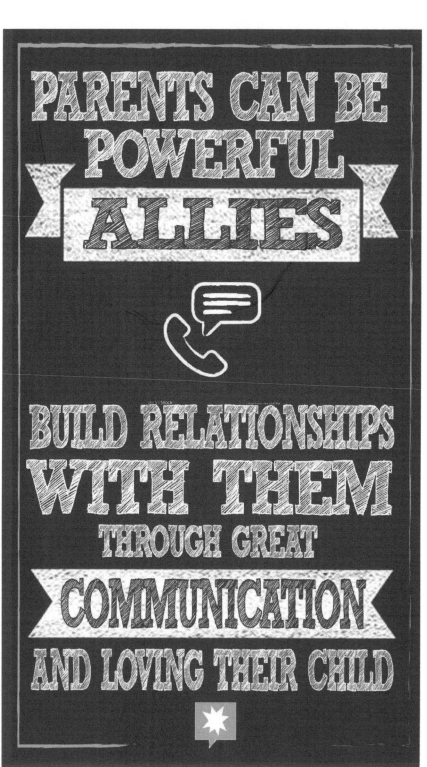

Make positive calls

Parents need to know that you care about their children and that they are succeeding under your care. When a student tries really hard, achieves a breakthrough or does something kind, pass that on to the parents. They will be very appreciative. This also has a positive impact on your relationship with the students and will bring you joy while making the call.

Be proactive

Parents do not like to be the last to know. Try your best to keep them in the loop as soon as problems start to arise. It is better to express concern at the beginning, than it is to wait until something negative occurs. This will let them know that you are on top of trying to improve the situation and hopefully, they will help you to work toward a solution.

Be professional

Ensure that your conversations with parents focus directly on their student. Respect the confidentiality of other students when meeting with parents. The last thing you need is another parent getting upset over information that you shared.

Make learning visible

Creating an engaging space for students to learn in is beneficial for many reasons. Your classroom says a lot about who you are as an educator. Make a great impression on parents by showcasing all of the amazing learning that is happening each day. Take pride in this space and invite parents into it with confidence.

Encourage your students to share at home

The best way to promote yourself as a great educator to parents is through the students. Work hard to make the students feel welcomed, safe, and connected to the learning in the classroom. Hopefully, they will share at home how great of an experience they are having, and that will help strengthen the trust and confidence that parents have in you.

Please note, even if you do everything right, some parents will still not be happy. Like everyone, parents come with their own experiences and perceptions. If a parent had a negative experience as a student or with other teachers, that might impact their attitude toward education and potentially you. Other parents struggle with anxiety and trust issues. Some parents are just unreasonable. Keep this in mind when these relationships are not developing as you would like. Try not to take it personally and continue to do what is best for the student.

WORK SMARTER, NOT HARDER

It is easy to never disconnect from work as an educator. Between planning, marking, extracurriculars, parent communication, professional development, emails, and meetings, you can easily fill every second of the day. This profession can swallow up even the most motivated and energetic person if you let it.

According to the National Education Association, in 2018, teachers in the United States worked an average of 50 hours per week. Approximately, 11 of these hours were spent on non-compensated school related activities.[135] In my opinion, these are acceptable statistics. It shows our dedication to our students and still gives us enough time outside of teaching to enjoy other aspects of our lives.

My concern is that in order to average out at 50 hours per week as a profession, that means there are many teachers who are putting in many more hours. These teachers have the best intentions in mind, but lose themselves in the constant workflow of education. Over time, this can lead to burn out and resentment if they are not careful.

Striving to find an appropriate work/life balance can be a challenge for many educators. However, there are things that we can do to ensure that we maintain our levels of motivation and happiness in this profession.

SAY NO!

Learning when and how to say 'No' is an important skill to learn in education. There are always going to be initiatives for us to take part in. Be very selective when it comes to committing your time to projects. We all need to do our part to make sure that the school meets the students' needs. The key is committing to things that you are most passionate about, and not getting pulled into things that you are not interested in.

My neighbor has the best strategies for creating space when asked to do something. Every time we ask her to babysit, she will say, "Let me check and get back to you." She rarely commits on the spot. This gives her enough time to think about if she really wants to do it or not. We really appreciate that she does this because when she commits we know that she is excited to help out.

Stay in Your Lane

One of my favorite administrators used to always remind me to stay in my lane. This was her way of cautioning me that I was beginning to wander from my goals and starting to spread myself thin. It is easy to do in education. Work on setting specific goals and sticking to the plans that you create. Being in too many different lanes makes it difficult to enjoy the ride.

Workaholic is Not a Badge of Honor

Many educators take a great deal of pride in how hard they work. That is a good thing. However, losing control of work/life balance should not be something we are proud of or something that is praised. In the long run, this will have a negative impact on our lives and our careers. To increase our teacher longevity, we need to work at investing our time wisely and finding that elusive thing we call balance.

Honor Time Set Aside For You

To ensure that you find work-life balance, set aside time to do things that you are passionate about outside of education. For some that might be uninterrupted family time, hobbies, recreational activities or time to work on passion projects. Honor that time as being extremely valuable.

For instance, when I decided to write this book, I set aside three or four nights a week after my kids went to bed. In the other evenings, I would spend time with my wife or friends socializing. It would have been easier to work on this every night; however, over time, I might begin to resent it. As I near completion of my first draft, I can honestly say that I have enjoyed every night of writing and never felt that I was missing out.

Toxicity Trap

I have the opportunity to visit many schools and sit in many different staff rooms. It would surprise you how many times I get a heads up on what table not to sit at during lunch. Unfortunately, negative people are drawn to each other. They will often spend their free time venting their frustrations. This is not a healthy way to spend your breaks.

To develop a more positive outlook, we should try investing our free time with people who reduce our stress and focus on the great things that are occurring. This is not to say that if someone is having a bad day, that we do not talk about it. That is important. However, the goal is to lift each other up, not to join in each other's misery.

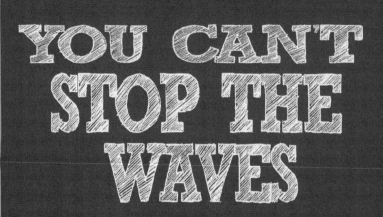

YOU CAN'T STOP THE WAVES

BUT YOU CAN LEARN TO SURF

- JON KABAT-ZINN

From experience, toxicity on staff can snowball quickly. The more people that join in, the worse it gets. Before you know it, everything is focused around the negative, and this is very draining. The sad part is that a lot of energy is invested, but very rarely does it lead to a solution.

My journey to find more happiness has given me a way out of these conversations. Now when I am getting pulled into negative rants, I politely say, "I am really working hard on staying more positive. Sorry, but I cannot keep engaging in conversations around this." Overall, I find people's reactions to this to be positive. In several situations, it has even helped these people realize the negative effect it is having on them.

Simply avoiding negative people is not the answer. Instead, try to help them become more positive. Often in education, we wait for a change in culture. Rarely do we realize that we can be this change. Start with surrounding yourself with positive people on staff. From there, try to shift those who are on the fence over to the positive side. If you are ambitious, make it your goal to help someone that is struggling. Happiness is contagious, so spread as much of it as possible!

LEARN TO SURF

Throughout our careers, we will witness many decisions and changes in directions that we do not agree with. Education is a complex system and one that can be difficult to be a part of at times. Sometimes decisions that are made at the top do not align with what we know is best for our students in the classroom. We must continue to voice our opinions and take stands when it jeopardizes the success and well-being of our students.

Saying that, it is also important that we do not develop a habit of engaging in continuous battles with the system throughout our career. In my opinion, this is the quickest way to become jaded and unhappy in education. We must learn to pick our battles carefully and find ways to make the best of the decisions that are being made.

"You can't stop the waves, but you can learn to surf." This is one of my favorite quotes relating to navigating system-level changes in education. From experience, I realized that engaging in endless battles with something that I cannot stop is exhausting. We need to learn to step back, think creatively about the situation, then maybe we can find a positive solution that makes it work for us.

Accept the ebb and flow of the educational system. Know that there will be good years and there will be bad years. Avoid settling into the idea that what is happening now is permanent. With new government comes

new solutions and issues. Focus on what you can control. Set your sights on providing the best education for your students relative to the situation that you are in. Work on being the light for others during the tough times and fight to maintain your love of teaching regardless of the politics.

More Stress Please

How do you think that stress impacts your health? This is a critical question to ask yourself, as it could determine how long you live. The way in which we frame stress can have a significant impact on the effect it will have on us.

Using research from the National Health Interview Survey (NHIS), Harvard researchers found that reframing stress as helpful rather than harmful can reverse the physiological changes that stress can have on our bodies. Not only that, it has also been shown to improve overall performance.

Here are some of the findings from this study of almost 30,000 participants:[136]

- Those who reported experiencing high stress and believed it was harmful had a 43% increase in risk of premature death.

- Those who reported experiencing high stress, but did not see it as harmful, were at the lowest risk of premature death- even lower than people who reported low stress.

We know we are going to encounter stress throughout our careers as educators. We must embrace stress and work on seeing it as something that will make us stronger and more viable. This will help us live successfully under all conditions that we may face in education.

Estimate your level of stress on the number line below. Reflect on how these different aspects of education impact your happiness in education.

OVERALL

Low   High

PLANNING AND LESSON DELIVERY

Low   High

STUDENTS

Low   High

PARENTS

Low   High

STAFF/ADMINSTRATION

Low   High

PROFESSIONAL DEVELOPMENT

Low   High

PERSONAL LIFE

Low   High

EXTRAORDINARY

"Wherever you find something extraordinary,
you'll find the fingerprints of a great teacher."
— *Arne Duncan*

I was waiting in line at a bakery when the cashier blurted to the customer in front of me, "Are you Mrs. Smith?"

The older lady slowly looked at her, smiled and said, "Yes, I am Dorthy. I can't believe you still remember me, it has been almost 50 years."

The cashier replied, "How could I not? You were my favorite teacher."

For the next couple of minutes I listened to them reminisce about memories they shared. The cashier even recalled the name and the scent of the perfume that Mrs. Smith used to wear while teaching. They apologized for taking so long to put through the order. I mentioned to them that I am a teacher and how much I enjoyed watching them reunite after all those years. It was a truly beautiful moment.

There was something about Mrs. Smith that made her so memorable. During her time in the classroom, she did something special that ingrained her memory into the hearts and minds of her students. You could tell by the cashier's reaction that Mrs. Smith was no ordinary teacher, she must have been extraordinary.

As I watched Mrs. Smith leave the bakery smiling ear-to-ear, it reinforced to me the importance of striving to always be our best as educators. It is our privilege to have the opportunity to make such a difference in people's lives and to find true fulfillment in our careers. We must not squander it by settling for mediocrity.

How is the View?

The Latin root of the word mediocre means, 'Middle of a Rugged Mountain.' That is not where we want to be in education. It is uncomfortable, lonely, and demoralizing. We need to convince ourselves that if we keep striving, we will eventually reach the summit. From there, we will feel empowered as we look back on our journey and feel grateful looking forward.

The opposite of mediocrity is extraordinary. As educators, that should be our goal. Like Mrs. Smith, we need to find a way to make an incredible impact on our students and the profession. Each route to get there will be different as we will rely on our strengths and our unique abilities. The key is to never stop trying to get better and be better for our students.

Level Four

Several years into my teaching career, I was having a conversation with one of my best friends from high school about how assessment had changed in education. He was just starting his career in business marketing, but always seemed to have a keen interest in education. I was explaining to him what a rubric was and how we use it to mark more efficiently. He was intrigued as he had never seen one before.

At one point in the conversation, I was explaining to him that a Level Four on a rubric meant that you went above and beyond the expectations. Being in marketing, he loved the conciseness of this terminology and what it represented. To this day, we still use Level Four as a way to let the other person know when they have exceeded expectations and done something amazing.

We also realized that we could apply the same principle of getting a Level Four to our own evaluation of ourselves. This became our mantra for self-improvement. Regardless of the task, we aim to go above and beyond the expectation that we set out for ourselves. This ensures that we are continually growing and pushing to get better.

For instance, I really enjoy video editing. My daughter's first Halloween, I decided to make a corny family movie on a whim. It was simple, but very cute. The next year, I wanted to Level Four it. So, I wrote a script. The following year, I began playing around with special effects. Now I am at the point where I am using a blue and green screen simultaneously to try to recreate scenes from the movie, Inside Out. A little crazy, but fun!

I truly believe that developing a personal Level Four philosophy is a great way to stay happy and motivated in education. When we shift our focus from impressing others to impressing ourselves, we are in control. We are no longer relying on the students, parents, and/or administration to recognize our efforts; we are doing it for ourselves. As long as we exceed our own expectations, that is all that should matter.

Adopting this mindset can be very freeing and motivating. There is a thrill that comes along with impressing yourself. You are proud, excited, and rejuvenated by the experience. You begin to crave more opportunities to impress yourself and to do things that you have never accomplished before.

Avoid trying to be the best. Instead just focus on being better and making those around you better. When we start competing with others, we limit our potential, and we limit the impact that we are having in education. Investing our energy in continual self-improvement is the key to becoming the educators that we set out to be in the beginning. Strive for your personal Level Four!

There is No Formula

I would love nothing more than to fill this chapter with ideas on how to become an even more extraordinary educator. However, it is not that simple. Becoming a teacher like Mrs. Smith is not something that anyone can teach you. It is something that only you can discover. The teachers that we remember so fondly found a way into our hearts by becoming the best versions of themselves and sharing their passion for education with us.

This being said, I do believe that many of these educators share many commonalities in the way that they approach education. Here are just some of the similarities they share:

- They believe that what they do every day matters and that they have the ability to change lives. They don't give up on either themselves or their students.

- They love deeply. Their students are more like family to them than they are students. They are as fond of their students as their students are of them.

- They go above and beyond in any way possible to support their students. Whether that means extra support in the classroom or giving up their personal time, they will be there if needed.

- They make memories. They want their students to look back and remember all of the great times they shared together.

- They make learning fun and exciting. They find ways to deliver content to students in a way that they can relate to and enjoy.

- They are resourceful and will let nothing stand in the way of providing their students with the quality of education they deserve (i.e. grants, fundraising, crowdfunding, etc.).

- They learn endlessly. They always want to be better for themselves and their students, and they know that the best way is to never stop learning.

- They never forget WHY they wanted to become an educator. They hold on tightly to this and allow it to drive everything that they do.

- They are happy. They love their jobs.

BE THAT TEACHER

Your students deserve a teacher at the front of the room that loves coming to work every day. Someone who is happy, passionate, caring and kind. Someone who inspires and leads. Someone who wants to make the world a better place. Someone who is extraordinary in their eyes. Someone they will never forget. Seize the opportunity and be that teacher.

And when you do, remember that you deserve it. You deserve to love going to work each day. You deserve having students who love and respect you. You deserve to be celebrated and recognized. You deserve feeling fulfilled. You deserve to look back on your career and know that you chose the right profession. Most of all, you deserve to be happy in education!

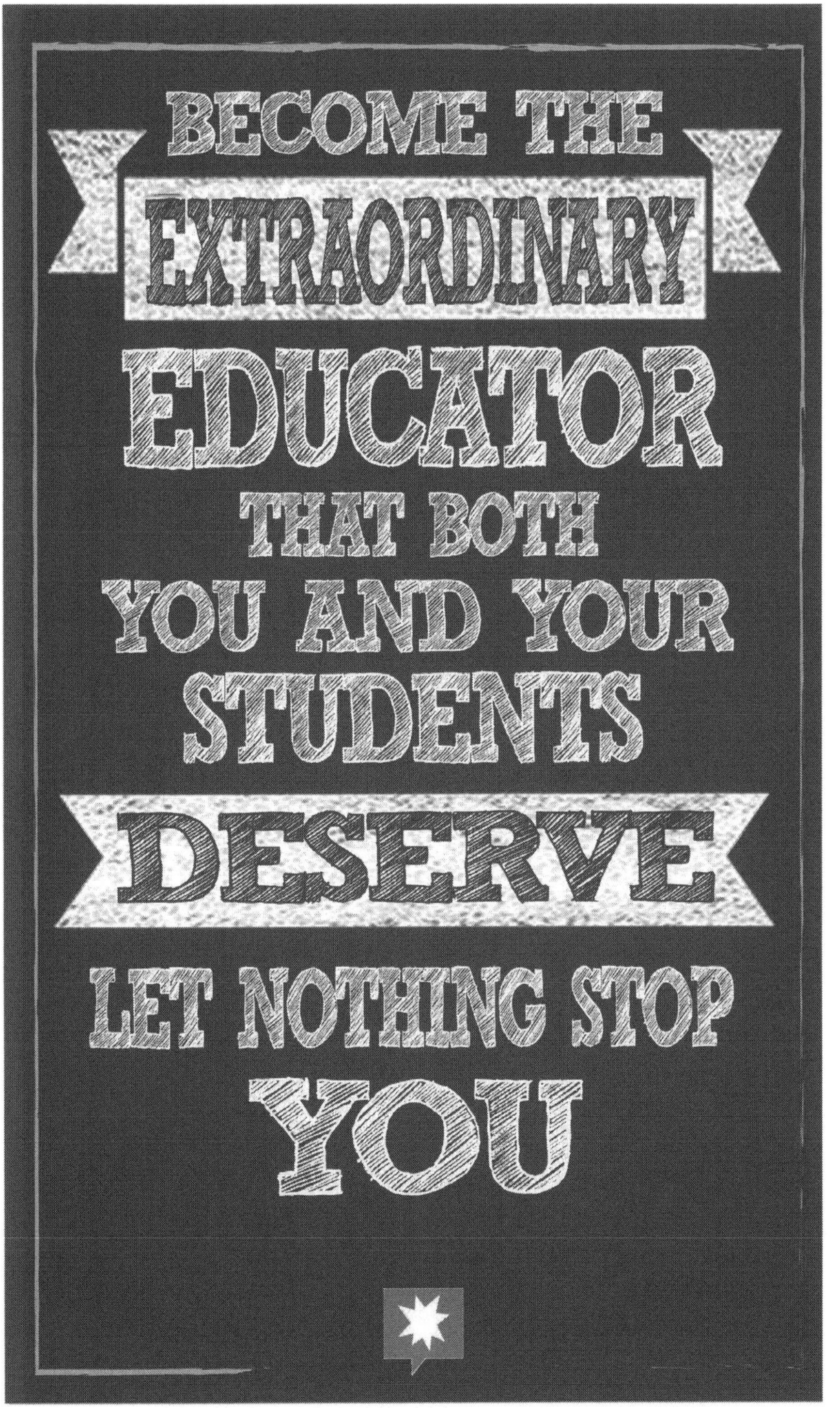
BECOME THE
EXTRAORDINARY
EDUCATOR
THAT BOTH
YOU AND YOUR
STUDENTS
DESERVE
LET NOTHING STOP
YOU

Acknowledgments

What a journey writing this book has been. Not only have I found more happiness in all aspects of my life, I have developed an even stronger appreciation for those who love and support me.

I would like to start off by saying thank you to my Mom and Dad who raised me to work hard and to be myself. The confidence they instilled in me at a young age played a crucial role in putting my ideas out into the world. I love you both to the moon and back.

To my sister Laura, who has always been my guiding light. I followed in your footsteps and you are the reason I became an educator. I admire the undying commitment you have for your students, friends and family. You are a truly inspirational educator and the best sister I could ask for. 🤟

To my amazing wife Melissa, who I fell in love with at first sight. Meeting you has made me a better person and I would not want to share my life with anyone but you. Without your support and all that you do for us, this book would not be possible. Thank you so much, I love you.

To my awesome kids, Lauren and Reid. You bring me happiness everyday. My gratitude app is filled with memories we share and things I love about both of you. Being your dad will always be my greatest accomplishment and the highlight of my life. Love Dad!

To Jon White. Meeting you in grade nine was a turning point in my life. I know that life would not be as good if we had not met. Love you brother.

To Neil Sarin, my level four partner in crime. You always saw something in me that I could not see. What a ride life has been with you by my side! Can't wait to make more memories.

To Micheal Snow, who came out of nowhere to become such a huge part of my life. Our win-win friendship and your ongoing support has meant so much to me and I am extremely grateful that I was your associate teacher.

To Melissa Mckinney-Lepp, Lee Martin, Jim Reschke and Kyle Kitchen. You are the epitome of TFFs to me. Working alongside you has changed me. Each of you are so talented, creative, student focussed and impactful educators. It has been my utmost pleasure to learn from you and develop a friendshp that will last a lifetime.

To teachers like Wendy Bilinski and John Haeni, who have shown me that it is possible to love being an educator throughout my entire career and beyond. Both of you have had an incredible impact on my life.

To my PLN and friends outside of education. I am grateful to have you as part of my life. I feel so fortunate to be able to reach out to you and share experiences with you.

Thanks to Shawn, Lea, Patrice, Kelly, Kim, Mike, Melissa, Wendy, Lee, and Kally for taking time out of your busy schedules to review my book. Your feedback was amazing! Thank you to Ryan for working on logo, cover design and illustrations. You are so talented.

To Edumatch who made my dream of publishing this book possible. Thank you to Sarah Thomas, Mandy Froehlich and everyone who helped with the editing and design of this book. Such a great publishing family to be a part of.

Finally, to all of the educators that I have worked with throughout the years. I have truly enjoyed getting to know and learn with you. What you do everyday matters and changes lives!

NOTES

PREFACE

1   "What Is SEL?" Casel, casel.org/what-is-sel/.
2   Durlak, Joseph A, et al. "The Impact of Enhancing Students' Social and Emotional Learning: a Meta-Analysis of School-Based Universal Interventions." Child Development, U.S. National Library of Medicine, 2011, www.ncbi.nlm.nih.gov/pubmed/21291449.
3   Lyubomirsky, Sonja. The How of Happiness: a Practical Guide to Getting the Life You Want. Piatkus, 2013.

PART ONE: HAPPINESS

THE POWER OF HAPPINESS

4   Tanza Loudenback, Emmie Martin. "13 Of the Happiest Companies in America." Business Insider, Business Insider, 29 Apr. 2016, www.businessinsider.com/payscale-best-companies-with-happiest-employees-in-america-2016-4#10-chevron-4.
5   Horton, Anisa Purbasari, and Anisa Purbasari Horton. "Employers, Your Idea about Employee Happiness Is All Wrong." Fast Company, Fast Company, 8 June 2018, www.fastcompany.com/40582655/employers-your-idea-about-employee-happiness-is-all-wrong.
6   "Toni: What Culture Means to Me." Zappos Insights, https://www.zapposinsights.com/blog/item/toni-what-culture-means-to-me.
7   Achor, Shawn. "The Happiness Dividend." Harvard Business Review, 23 July 2014, hbr.org/2011/06/the-happiness-dividend.
8   Crum, A. J., Salovey, P., & Achor, S. (2013). Rethinking stress: The role of mindsets in determining the stress response. Journal of Personality and Social Psychology, 104(4), 716–733. doi: 10.1037/a0031201

9   Achor, Shawn. The Happiness Advantage: the Seven Principles That Fuel Success and Performance at Work. Virgin, 2011.

10   "College Faces Mental Health Crisis: News: The Harvard Crimson." College Faces Mental Health Crisis | News, www.thecrimson.com/article/2004/1/12/college-faces-mental-health-crisis-one/.

11   "Positive Psychology 1504: Harvard's Groundbreaking Course." PositivePsychology.com, 12 July 2019, positivepsychology.com/harvard-positive- psychology-course-1504/.

12   Crabtree, Steve. "Worldwide, 13% of Employees Are Engaged at Work." Gallup.com, Gallup, 16 May 2019, news.gallup.com/poll/165269/worldwide-employees-engaged -work.aspx.

Preparing For Happiness

13   Markowsky, George. "Information Theory." Encyclopædia Britannica, Encyclopædia Britannica, Inc., 16 June 2017, www.britannica.com/science/information-theory/Physiology.

14   Achor, Shawn. Before Happiness: the 5 Hidden Keys to Achieving Success, Spreading Happiness, and Sustaining Positive Change. Crown Business, 2013.

15   Sinek, Simon. "How Great Leaders Inspire Action." TED, www.ted.com/talks/simon_sinek_how_great_leaders_inspire_action?language=en.

16   García Héctor, et al. Ikigai: the Japanese Secret to a Long and Happy Life. Penguin Books, 2017.

17   "Okinawa, Japan." Blue Zones, www.bluezones.com/exploration/okinawa-japan/.

18   "Karate." VISIT OKINAWA JAPAN, www.visitokinawa.jp/information/karate.

Working Towards Happiness

19   "A Quote by Simon Sinek." Goodreads, Goodreads, www.goodreads.com/quotes/ 7697100-working-hard-for-something-we-don-t-care-about-is-called.

20   Killingsworth, Matt. "A Wandering Mind Is an Unhappy Mind." PsycEXTRA Dataset, 2011, doi:10.1037/e634112013-170.

21   Harris, Dan. 10% Happier: How I Tamed the Voice in My Head, Reduced Stress without Losing My Edge, and Found Self-Help That Actually Works--a True Story. Dey St., an Imprint of William Morris Publishers, 2014.

22 Blumenthal, James A, et al. "Is Exercise a Viable Treatment for Depression?" ACSM's Health & Fitness Journal, U.S. National Library of Medicine, July 2012, www.ncbi.nlm.nih.gov/pmc/articles/PMC3674785/.

23 Blumenthal, James A., et al. "Effects of Exercise Training on Older Patients With Major Depression." Archives of Internal Medicine, vol. 159, no. 19, 1999, doi:10.1001/archinte.159.19.2349.

24 Maslach, Christina, and Michael P. Leiter. "Understanding the Burnout Experience: Recent Research and Its Implications for Psychiatry." World Psychiatry, vol. 15, no. 2, 2016, pp. 103–111., doi:10.1002/wps.20311.

25 "Gratitude and Well-Being." Emmons Lab, emmons.faculty.ucdavis.edu/

PART TWO: STRIVE

Students

26 Couros, George. The Innovator's Mindset: Empower Learning, Unleash Talent, and Lead a Culture of Creativity. Dave Burgess Consulting, Inc., 2015.

27 Cook, Clayton R., et al. "Positive Greetings at the Door: Evaluation of a Low-Cost, High-Yield Proactive Classroom Management Strategy." Journal of Positive Behavior Interventions, vol. 20, no. 3, 2018, pp. 149–159., doi:10.1177/1098300717753831.

28 "Every Kid Is ONE Caring Adult Away from Being a Success Story... Says Former Foster Kid." Teen Expert Josh Shipp, 9 May 2019, joshshipp.com/one-caring-adult/.

Team

29 Rath, Tom, and James K. Harter. well-being: the Five Essential Elements. Gallup Press, 2014.

30 "Harvard Second Generation Study." Harvard Second Generation Study, www.adultdevelopmentstudy.org/.

31 Diener, Ed, and Martin E.p. Seligman. "Very Happy People." Psychological Science, vol. 13, no. 1, 2002, pp. 81–84., doi:10.1111/1467-9280.00415.

32 Achor, Shawn. The Happiness Advantage: the Seven Principles That Fuel Success and Performance at Work. Virgin, 2011.

33   Holt-Lunstad, Julianne, and Timothy Smith. "Social Relationships and Mortality Risk: A Meta-Analytic Review." SciVee, 2010, doi:10.4016/19911.01.

34   Carpenter, Derrick. "How Introverts Can Enhance Their Happiness." Verywell Mind, Verywell Mind, 24 June 2019, https://www.verywellmind.com/how-to-be-a-happy-introvert-1717557.

35   Margolis, Seth, and Sonja Lyubomirsky. "Experimental Manipulation of Extraverted and Introverted Behavior and Its Effects on Well-Being." Journal of Experimental Psychology: General, Jan. 2019, doi:10.1037/xge0000668.

36   "Power 9®." Blue Zones, 5 June 2019, www.bluezones.com/2016/11/power-9/.

37   Buettner, Dan/ Diener Ed (FRW). The Blue Zones of Happiness: Lessons from the WorldsHappiest People. Random House Inc, 2017.

38   "Dan Buettner's Lessons from the Happiest Places on Earth." The Globe and Mail, 23 Oct. 2017, www.theglobeandmail.com/life/health-and-fitness/health/dan-buettners- lessons-from-the-happiest-places-on-earth/article36667890/.

39   Byrne, Rhonda. The Secret. Atria Books, 2018.

40   Schwartz, Barry, and Barry Schwartz. "What's the Most Satisfying Job in the World? You'd Be Surprised." Ideas.ted.com, Ideas.ted.com, 18 Nov. 2015, ideas.ted.com/whats-the-most-satisfying-job-in-the-world-youd-be-surprised/.

41   Hall, Jeffrey A. "How Many Hours Does It Take to Make a Friend?" Journal of Social and Personal Relationships, vol. 36, no. 4, 2018, pp. 1278–1296., doi:10.1177/0265407518761225.

42   The Value of Extracurricular Activities Infographic - e-Learning Infographics." e, 20 Nov. 2014, elearninginfographics.com/value-extracurricular-activities-infographic/.

43   Moran, James. " May 2017, https://etd.ohiolink.edu/!etd.send_file?accession=ysu1492182067273518&disposition=inline.

44   Pinker, Susan. The Village Effect: Why Face-to-Face Contact Matters. Atlantic Books, 2015.

45   Asano, Evan. "How Much Time Do People Spend on Social Media? [Infographic]." Social Media Today, 4 Jan. 2017, www.socialmediatoday.com/marketing/ how-much- time-do-people-spend-social-media-infographic.

46   Nobel, Jeremy. "Does Social Media Make You Lonely?" Harvard Health Blog, 21 Dec. 2018, www.health.harvard.edu/blog/is-a-steady-diet-of-social-media-unhealthy- 2018122115600.

47   "Novel Research Approaches to Gauge Global Teacher Familiarity with Game-Based Teaching in Physical Education: an Exploratory #Twitter Analysis." Taylor & Francis, www.tandfonline.com/doi/full/10.1080/18377122.2017.1315953.

48   Arens, Elizabeth. "Best Times to Post on Social Media for 2019." Sprout Social, 8 July 2019, sproutsocial.com/insights/best-times-to-post-on-social-media/.

49   "Education Chats." Google Sites, sites.google.com/site/twittereducationchats/ education-chat-calendar.

Routines

50   Neal, D. T., Wood, W., & Quinn, J. M. (2006). Habits—A repeat performance.

51   "Does Commuting Affect Happiness & well-being?: The Happiness Index™." The Happiness Index, 9 Jan. 2017, thehappinessindex. com/blog/work-life-balance/ how-commuting-affects-well-being-happiness/.

52   Buettner, Dan. The Blue Zones of Happiness: a Blueprint for a Better Life. National Geographic, 2017.

53   Hjelmborg, J.., Iachine, I., Skytthe, A. et al. Hum Genet (2006) 119: 312.

54   "Blue Zones Results: Albert Lea, MN." Blue Zones, www.bluezones. com/blue-zones-results-albert-lea-mn/#section-2.

55   "Blue Zones Project®." Blue Zones, www.bluezones.com/services/blue-zones-project-old/#section-2.

56   "How Habits Work." Charles Duhigg, charlesduhigg.com/how-habits-work/.

57   Duhigg, Charles. The Power of Habit: Why We Do What We Do in Life and Business. Anchor Canada, 2014.

58   "Design Bite #1 - The Habit Loop - Big Tomorrow." Medium, Big Tomorrow, 21 Apr. 2017, medium.com/bigtomorrow/design-bite-1-the-habit-loop-ee79153de76c.

59   "The Science of How Habits Are Formed." Habit, habit.com/blog/2018/01/09/habits- formed-science-habit-loop/.

60   Duhigg, Charles. The Power of Habit: Why We Do What We Do in Life and Business. Anchor Canada, 2014.

61   "2 Essential Habits for Your Health and Happiness." Psychology Today, Sussex Publishers, www.psychologytoday.com/ca/blog/changepower/201501/2-essential-habits-your-health-and-happiness.

62   "Make Your Bed, Change Your Life?" Psychology Today, Sussex Publishers,https://www.psychologytoday.com/ca/blog/brain-candy/201208/make-your-bed-change-your-life.

63   Duhigg, Charles. The Power of Habit: Why We Do What We Do in Life and Business. Random House Trade Paperbacks, 2014.

64   Lally, Phillippa, et al. "How Are Habits Formed: Modeling Habit Formation in the Real World." European Journal of Social Psychology, vol. 40, no. 6, 2009, pp. 998–1009., doi:10.1002/ejsp.674.

65   Rae, Tina, and Ruth MacConville. Using Positive Psychology to Enhance Student Achievement: a Schools-Based Programme for Character Education. Routledge, 2015.

66   Dean, Jeremy. Making Habits, Breaking Habits: How to Make Changes That Stick. Oneworld, 2013.

67   BROWN, BRENE. BRAVING THE WILDERNESS: the Quest for True Belonging and the Courage to Stand Alone. RANDOM HOUSE, 2019.

68   "How Many Hours of Sleep Do You Need?" Mayo Clinic, Mayo Foundation for Medical Education and Research, 6 June 2019, www.mayoclinic.org/healthy-lifestyle/adult-health/expert-answers/how-many-hours-of-sleep-are-enough/faq-20057898.

69   Ransford, Marc. "Study Finds That Teachers Are Fighting to Stay Awake in the Classroom." Ball State University, www.bsu.edu/news/articles/2008/9/study-finds-that-teachers-are-fighting-

70   "How and Why Waking up at the Same Time Every Day Can Improve Your Health | CBC Life." CBCnews, CBC/Radio Canada, 7 Aug. 2018, www.cbc.ca/life/wellness/ how-and-why-waking-up-at-the-same-time-everyday-can-improve-your-health-1.4357391.

71   Drake, Christopher, et al. "Caffeine Effects on Sleep Taken 0, 3, or 6 Hours before Going to Bed." Journal of Clinical Sleep Medicine : JCSM : Official Publication of the American Academy of Sleep Medicine, American Academy of Sleep Medicine, 15 Nov. 2013, www.ncbi.nlm.nih.gov/pmc/articles/PMC3805807/.

72   "How Technology Impacts Sleep Quality." Sleep.org, www.sleep.org/articles/ ways-technology-affects-sleep/.

73   "S ResMed." Darkness Matters - How Light Affects Sleep, sleep.mysplus.com/library /category2/article1.html.

74   "Physical Activity Basics | Physical Activity | CDC." Centers for Disease Control and Prevention, Centers for Disease Control and Prevention, www.cdc.gov/physicalactivity/basics/index.htm.

75   Government of Ontario. "Healthy Schools: Daily Physical Activity." Untitled Document, Government of Ontario, www.edu.gov.on.ca/eng/healthyschools/dpa.html.

76   "Breakfast for Learning." Food Research & Action Center, frac.org/research /resource-library/breakfast-for-learning.

77   "How Many People Skip Breakfast." The NPD Group, www.npd.com/wps/portal/npd/us/news/press-releases/pr_111011b/.

78   "Eating 9 to 5." Dietitians of Canada, https://www.dietitians.ca/Downloads/Public/Fact_ Sheet_1_NM_2015_ENG_COL.aspx

79   Tenney, Matt. "4 Ways Mindfulness Improves Your Productivity." HuffPost, HuffPost, 7 Dec. 2017, www.huffpost.com/entry/4-ways-mindfulness-improv_b_9738720.

80   Wolever, Ruth Q., et al. "Effective and viable mind-body stress reduction in the workplace: a randomized controlled trial." Journal of occupational health psychology 17.2 (2012): 246.

81   "The True Cost Of Multi-Tasking." Psychology Today, SussexPublishers,www.psychologytoday.com/ca/blog/brainwise/201209/the-true-cost-multi-tasking.

82   Urry, Heather, et al. "Making a life worth living: neural correlates of well-being." Psychology Science. 2004 Jun;15(6):367-72.

83   Killingsworth, M. A. & Gilbert, D. T. (2010). A Wandering Mind is an Unhappy Mind. Science. 330(6006), p932.

84   Wegrich, Kyme, et al. "The Calm Schools Initiative." Calm, www.calm.com/schools.

85   "Relaxation Techniques: Try These Steps to Reduce Stress." Mayo Clinic, Mayo Foundation for Medical Education and Research, 19 Apr. 2017, www.mayoclinic.org /healthy-lifestyle/stress-management/in-depth/relaxation-technique/art-20045368.

86   Rahal, Louai. "How Gratitude and Mindfulness Go Hand in Hand." World of Psychology, 8 July 2018, psychcentral.com/blog/how-gratitude-and-mindfulness-go- hand-in-hand/.

87   Park, N., Peterson, C. & Seligman, M. (2004). Strengths of character and well-being. Journal of Social and Clinical Psychology, 23, 603–619.

88   "7 Scientifically Proven Benefits of Gratitude." Psychology Today, Sussex Publishers, www.psychologytoday.com/ca/blog/what-mentally-strong-people-dont-do/201504/7-scientifically-proven-benefits-gratitude.

89   "Daily Gratitude Journal App." *Happyfeed*, www.*happyfeed*.co/.

90 Pedro, et al. "The Impact of Studying Brain Plasticity." Frontiers, Frontiers, 11 Feb. 2019, www.frontiersin.org/articles/10.3389/fncel.2019.00066/full.

91 Seligman, Martin E. P. Learned Optimism. Nicholas Brealey Publishing, 2018.

92 Hanson, Rick. Hardwiring Happiness: the New Brain Science of Contentment, Calm, and Confidence. Harmony Books, 2013.

93 "Time Flies: U.S. Adults Now Spend Nearly Half a Day Interacting with Media." Nielsen, www.nielsen.com/us/en/insights/article/2018/time-flies-us-adults-now-spend-nearly-half-a-day-interacting-with-media/

94 Gielan, M. & Achor, S. "Consuming Negative News Can Make You Less Effective at Work." Harvard Business Review, 28 Dec. 2015, hbr.org/2015/09/consuming-negative-news-can-make-you-less-effective-at-work.

95 "Nielsen: Podcast Numbers Continue to Add Up for Brands." Insideradio.com, 26 June 2017, www.insideradio.com/free/nielsen-podcast-numbers-continue-to-add-up-for-brands/article_2d982bdc-5a3f-11e7-8fec-3f0a02151f30.html.

96 "Cult of Pedagogy." Cult of Pedagogy, www.cultofpedagogy.com/.

97 Raphael, T.J. "The World Is Actually Safer than Ever. And Here's the Data to Prove That." Jefferson Public Radio, https://www.ijpr.org/post/world-actually- safer-ever-and -heres-data-prove#stream/0.

98 "Policy Definition and Meaning: Collins English Dictionary." Policy Definition and Meaning | Collins English Dictionary, www.collinsdictionary.com/ dictionary/english/ policy.

99 "Face-to-Face Contacts (Not Facebook Connections), Impact Your Health and Longevity." Blue Zones, 18 Dec. 2018, www.bluezones.com/2017/10/face-face-interactions-not-facebook-connections-impact-health-longevity/.

100 Holt-Lunstad, Julianne, et al. "Loneliness and Social Isolation as Risk Factors for Mortality." Perspectives on Psychological Science, vol. 10, no. 2, 2015, pp. 227–237., doi:10.1177/1745691614568352.

101 Pinker, Susan. The Village Effect: Why Face-to-Face Contact Matters. Atlantic Books, 2015.

102 Pinker, Susan. "The Secret to Living Longer May Be Your Social Life." TED, www.ted.com/talks/susan_pinker_the_secret_to_living_longer_may_be_your_social_life?language=en.

103 "Dan Buettner's Lessons from the Happiest Places on Earth." The Globe and Mail, 23 Oct. 2017, www.theglobeandmail.com/life/health-and-fitness/health/dan-buettners-lessons-from-the-happiest-places-on-earth/article36667890/.

104 MacGill, Markus. "Oxytocin: The Love Hormone?" Medical News Today, MediLexicon International, 4 Sept. 2017, www.medicalnewstoday.com/articles/275795.php.

105 Sorenson, Susan. "How Employees' Strengths Make Your Company Stronger." Gallup.com, Gallup, 30 May 2019, news.gallup.com/businessjournal/167462/employees-strengths-company-stronger.aspx.

106 "Unlock Your Children's Potential by Helping Them Build Their Strengths." Strength Switch, https://www.strengthswitch.com/.

107 "The VIA Character Strengths Survey." Personality Test, Personality Assessment: VIA Survey | VIA Institute, www.viacharacter.org/Survey/Account/Register.

108 "The 24 Character Strengths." Find Your 24 Character Strengths | Personal Strengths List | VIA Institute, https://www.viacharacter.org/character-strengths.

109 Csikszentmihalyi, Mihaly. Flow: the Psychology of Optimal Experience. Harper Row, 2009.

110 "8 Ways To Create Flow According to Mihaly Csikszentmihalyi [TEDTalk]."PositivePsychology.com, 4July2019, positivepsychology.com/mihaly-csikszentmihalyi-father-of-flow/#flow-types-characteristics.

111 Seligman, Martin E. P. Flourish: a Visionary New Understanding of Happiness and Well-Being. Atria, 2013.

112 Nguyen. "Hacking Into Your Happy Chemicals: Dopamine, Serotonin, Endorphins and Oxytocin." HuffPost, HuffPost, 7 Dec. 2017, www.huffpost.com/entry/hacking-into-your-happy-c_b_6007660.

113 Cohut, Maria. "Serotonin Enhances Learning, Not Just Mood." Medical News Today, MediLexicon International, 26 June 2018, www.medicalnewstoday.com/articles/322263.php.

114 Roman, Kaia. "How to Trigger the Brain Chemicals That Make You Happy." Medium, Thrive Global, 15 July 2017, https://medium.com/thrive-global/the-brain-chemicals-that-make-you-happy-and-how-to-trigger-them-caa5268eb2c.

115 Carter, Christine. Raising Happiness: 10 Simple Steps for More Joyful Kids and Happier Parents. Ballantine Books, 2011.

116 Walsh, Colleen, and Colleen Walsh. "Money Spent on Others Can Buy Happiness." Harvard Gazette, Harvard Gazette, 17 Apr. 2008, news.harvard.edu/gazette/story/2008/04/money-spent-on-others-can-buy-happiness/.

117 "Make Kindness The Norm." Random Acts of Kindness, www.randomactsofkindness.org/the-science-of-kindness.

118 Layous, Kristin, et al. "Kindness Counts: Prompting Prosocial Behavior in Preadolescents Boosts Peer Acceptance and Well-Being." PloS One, Public Library of Science, 26 Dec. 2012, www.ncbi.nlm.nih.gov/pmc/articles/PMC3530573/.

119 Changes in Dispositional Empathy in American College ...faculty.chicagobooth.edu/eob/edobrien_empathyPSPR.pdf.

INNOVATE

120 "Innovation." Merriam-Webster, Merriam-Webster, www.merriam-webster.com/dictionary/innovation.

121 Brown, Claire. "How Better Note Taking Can Improve Your Memory." World Economic Forum, www.weforum.org/agenda/2015/05/whats-the-most-effective -way-to-take-notes/.

122 "Why Generation Z Learners Prefer YouTube Lessons Over Printed Books." New Tech Network, 20 Sept. 2018, newtechnetwork.org/resources/why-generation-z-learners-prefer-youtube-lessons-over-printed-books/.

123 Drive: The Surprising Truth About What Motivates Us. Riverhead Books,U.S., 2013.

VIABILITY

124 Viability"Viability." Dictionary.com, Dictionary.com, www.dictionary.com/browse/viability.

125 Johnson, Spencer. Peaks and Valleys: Making Good and Bad Times Work for You - at Work and in Life. Simon & Schuster, 2014.

126 Charles R. Swindoll Quotes (Author of The Grace Awakening)." Goodreads, Goodreads, www.goodreads.com/author/quotes/5139.Charles_R_Swindoll.

127 Seligman, Martin E. P. Learned Optimism: How to Change Your Mind and Your Life. Vintage, 2006.

128 Seligman, Martin E. P. Learned Optimism: How to Change Your Mind and Your Life. Vintage, 2006.

129   Seligman, Martin E. P. Learned Optimism: How to Change Your Mind and Your Life. Vintage, 2006.

130   Talks, TEDx. "What Are You Practicing Right Now? | Dave Mochel | TEDxPasadenaWomen." YouTube, YouTube, 22 Nov. 2016, www.youtube.com/watch?v=AkXA8rgqiss.

131   Marable, Manning, and Leith Mullings. Let Nobody Turn Us around: Voices of Resistance, Reform, and Renewal ; an African American Anthology. Rowman & Littlefield Publishers, Inc., 2009.

132   Weale, Sally. "Fifth of Teachers Plan to Leave Profession within Two Years." The Guardian, Guardian News and Media, 15 Apr. 2019, www.theguardian.com/education/2019/apr/16/fifth-of-teachers-plan-to-leave-profession-within-two-years.

133   "Teacher Stress and Health." RWJF, 31 Jan. 2018, www.rwjf.org/en/library/research/2016/07/teacher-stress-and-health.html.

134   "Are You Suffering from Compassion Fatigue?" Psychology Today, Sussex Publishers, www.psychologytoday.com/ca/blog/high-octane-women/201407/ are-you-suffering-compassion-fatigue.

135   Higley, Danielle. "New Data Shows Educators Work 11 Hours Overtime per Week." The Time Tracking Blog, 8 May 2018, blog.tsheets.com/2018/news/teacher-appreciation-day.

136   Keller, Abiola, et al. "Does the Perception That Stress Affects Health Matter? The Association with Health and Mortality." Health Psychology : Official Journal of the Division of Health Psychology, American Psychological Association, U.S. National Library of Medicine, Sept. 2012, www.ncbi.nlm.nih.gov/pmc/articles/PMC3374921/.. 2012, www.ncbi.nlm.nih.gov/pmc/articles/PMC3374921/.

Index

A

Access to Global Support 88
Active Duty 115
Active Listening Skills 76
activity goals 115
altruistic 37, 171
Annual Learning Plan 81, 195
audiobooks 100, 139, 141
Authentic 65, 195

B

Bedtime Routine 131
Before Happiness 27, 238
Be Kind Online 172
belief statements 25, 28
Blogging 93
Blue Zone 147
Book Clubs 151
Breakfast 118, 127, 243
Breakfast Program for Educators 118
Breakthrough 69
Breathing 127, 129
Brene Brown 113
Buddy Bench 173
burnout 37, 125, 217, 218

C

Caffeine 114, 242
Care For Yourself 179
Centre for Disease Control 115

Chad-Meng Tan 19
Change is Necessary 185
Charles Duhigg 102, 104, 241

Chief Happiness Officers 19, 20
Choose Kind 171
Clubs 163
Coaching 163
Compassion Overload 217
Compliment Yourself 177
Confidence 63, 244
Co-Teaching 152
Create a Profile 62
creativity 21, 22, 67, 153, 188
cues 103
Curriculum To Grow 198

D

Daily Physical Activity Policy 117
daily routine 99, 103
Dan Buettner 73
Dan Harris 36
David Mochel 214
Decorate With Kindness 173
Detach From Work 37
Distractions 166, 198
Do Not Disturb 114
Dopamine 169, 245
Dotmocracy 48
Dr. Lea Waters 157
Dr. Ritchie Davidson 171
Duke SMILE 36

E

Educator Outings 150
Effective Feedback 202
emotional well-being 36, 39, 150, 171
energy levels 21
engaged at work 23

Engage Senses 129
Everyday Gestures 179
Exercise 36, 131, 239
Explanatory Style 207
Extracurriculars 48
Extraordinary 229

F

face-to-face 73, 85, 88, 94, 95, 147
Fan Their Passions 202
Fear 65
Filling in the Gaps 63
First Impression 90
Flexibility 88
Flow 161, 162, 163, 165, 167, 245
Forgive Yourself 177
Free Gym Membership 115

G

Gallup 23, 71, 238, 239, 245
Genius Hour 51, 166
George Curous 37
Give Yourself a Break 179
Golden Circle. 30
Golden Rule of Habit Change 103
Gratitude 37, 131, 132, 133, 159, 239, 243
Gratitude App 132
Gratitude Exit Cards 133
Gratitude Journals 131
Gratitude Stations 133
Great Kindness Challenge 175
Great Parking Spot 127

H

habit loop 102
Habit Pairing 103
habituation 105
Happiness Advantage 22, 23, 238, 239
Happiness Prescription 35
Happiness Timeline 206
Happiness Trifecta 169
Happyfeed 132, 211, 243
Harvard 20, 22, 23, 54, 71, 72, 126, 138, 171, 227, 237, 238, 239, 240, 244,
246
Higher Sales 22
Hold Ideas Lightly 183
How of Happiness 15

I

icebreaker 46, 48
Ikigai 30, 31, 43, 238
Innovate Your Career 183
Intensity Versus Consistency 213
Intrinsic Motivation 166
Introverts 72, 240
Invest In Yourself 75

J

Jeremy Dean 107

K

Keystone Habits 104
Kindness 79, 159, 171, 172, 173, 175, 246
KINDNESS AS A SCHOOL 173
Kindness Bingo 172
Kindness Calendar 172
Kindness Class Code 172
Kindness is Teachable 171
KINDNESS ON STAFF 175
Kindness Snowball Fight 172
KINDNESS TO YOURSELF 176

L

leadership 19, 39, 137, 165, 186
leaf focussed 13
Learned Optimism 207
Learn to Surf 225
Leisure Activities 165
Level Four 230, 231
life satisfaction 15, 37
Listen to Your Life 183

M

Martin Seligman 72, 157, 159, 207
Meal Plan 119
Media 89, 138, 143, 240, 241, 244, 247

media consumption 137, 143
Meditation 129
Meet a Hero 143
Mentoring 153
meta-analysis study 147
Mihaly Csikszentmihalyi 162, 245
Mindful Breakfast 127
Mindfulness 36, 126, 129, 130, 243
Mindfulness Inquiry 129
Mindset 43, 239
Monitor Progress 166
Mortality Risks Study 72
motivation 14, 15, 23, 29, 37, 141, 162, 166, 169, 195, 222
Motivation Mondays 142
Movement Breaks 117
multitasking 126

N

negativity bias 138
neuroplasticity 137
New Learning Culture 201
nudge 101, 142, 147, 151, 196
NUTRITION 118

O

Okinawans 31
Online Chat 93
Open Invites 51, 52
optimistic 35, 87, 132, 137, 209
Oxytocin 169, 245

P

parent communication 219, 222
Passion Portfolios 49, 51
Peaks and Valleys 7, 205, 206, 246
peer acceptance 171
perception 25, 27, 125, 137, 196
performance 13, 37, 46, 75, 125, 199, 217, 227, 241
Permanence 207, 209
Permission 111, 113
Permission Slips 113
Personalization 207
Personal Learning Network 85, 87, 89, 95, 198
Pervasiveness 207
phoropter 33
PHYSICAL ACTIVITY 115
Physical Triggers 130
Pick One 47
Playlist 141
Podcast 139, 244
positive calls 221
Positive Intake 143
Positive Media Literacy Unit 143
positive mindset 21, 45, 137
Positive News Wall 142
positive psychology 15, 20, 39, 71, 72
Positive Reality 27, 28
Positivity Policy 145
Powerful Password 130
Power of Habits 102
prefrontal cortex 126
Productive 20
Productivity Trap 125
professional development 87, 88, 152, 188, 195, 196, 197, 198, 222
Professional Friendship Development 152
Profile 62, 157
Progress equals happiness 193
psychology 15, 20, 39, 71, 72, 161, 238, 243
Pump Yourself Up 177

Q

Quick Chats 47

R

Random Acts of Recognition 79, 80, 102
Recognition 77, 79, 80, 102
relationships 13, 20, 39, 43, 45, 49, 52, 53, 62, 71, 72, 75, 76, 77, 79, 80, 81, 88, 95, 118, 122, 131, 132, 137, 147, 149, 151, 155, 169, 175, 186, 209, 213, 219, 222
Remove Distractions 198
Resources 82
rewards 103, 105

Right Team 73
Robert Emmons 37
Robert Waldinger 72
root of the issue 13
Rotating Lunches 121
Routines 7, 99, 100, 109, 241

S

Savoring 135
Say No 222
Scaffolding 166, 202
Screen Curfew 114
Self-Worth 63
Serotonin 169, 245
Shawn Achor 22, 23, 27, 72
Shower Escape 127
Signature Skills 159, 160
Simon Sinek 29, 33, 238
SLEEP 113
SMILE 36
Social Catalyst Risk Taker 76
social-emotional learning 13
socializing 81
social media 85, 87, 88, 90, 91, 93, 94,
        95, 96, 138, 142
Social Niche 155
Sonja Lyubomenski 15
Spencer Johnson 205
Stand Up for Yourself 179
Stay Active 91
Stay in Your Lane 223
Strength Switch 157
Strive for 40 15
Student Hyper-Focus 45
Students to Grow 201
Study of Adult Development 71
subjective well-being 35
Summer Reboot 211
supportive adult 54
Survey 48, 49, 227, 245
Susan Pinker 147

T

Task-Switching 126
Teacher Clubs 149
Teacher Friends Forever 71, 77, 83,
        152, 177
Teacher Treasure Chest 143
Teaching Wall of Fame 145
Teach more Skills 201
Team TV Watching 152
TED talk 147
the 'zone' 161
Third-Party Compliment 173
Tony Hsieh 19
Toxicity 223
Trust 63, 66
Tweetups 94
Twitter 88, 90, 91, 94, 241

U

Unique Skill Set 75
Unwind 130
Using Students to Grow 201
Using the Curriculum To Grow 198

V

Very Happy People Study 72
Villagrande 147
Vision 65
Volunteering 165

W

well-being 19, 35, 36, 37, 39, 65, 71, 72,
        87, 100, 103, 104, 109, 111, 113,
        117, 118, 137, 138, 139, 141, 143,
        147, 150, 169, 171, 183, 187, 213,
        214, 218, 225, 239, 241, 243
Wendy Bilinski 14
What We Teach 188
When and How Much Change 189
Where We Teach 185
Who We Teach 187
WHY 30, 35, 232
Work Dates 151
work-life balance 217, 223

Z

zone 73, 161, 166, 185, 214

Robert Dunlop is a middle school teacher and technology consultant. His experiences in the classroom and throughout his district have given him a deep insight into the importance of teacher happiness. He credits working with thousands of educators as paramount to his research for this book. Robert's teaching journey has been one of peaks and valleys. His work in schools and his role in creating the Terry Fox Lesson Plans for educators around the world, led to him being honored with the Prime Minister's Award for Teaching Excellence. Although Robert has enjoyed many peaks throughout his career, he credits his valleys for his greatest learning. The message he shares in this book, online and through his speaking comes from his passion to reconnect to his love of teaching. Robert looks forward to inspiring many more educators to find Happiness in Education.

You can connect with Robert Dunlop using
the following social media handle
@robdunlopEDU

Made in the USA
Columbia, SC
14 March 2022

57342096R00139